FINE UNTIL KINDERGARTEN

CATHERINE MIKKELSEN

FINE UNTIL KINDERGARTEN

A Parent's First Guide to Learning Differences™

BrainParenting Books

BrainParenting books titles may be purchased for business or promotional use, or by parent groups or education institutions. For information, please email Promotions, at BrainParenting Books: Brainparenting@gmail.com

PRINTED IN THE UNITED STATES OF AMERICA

BRAINPARENTING is a Trademark.

Visit our website at www.fineuntilkindergarten.com/bonus for special bonus pages for our readers.

The author describes a variety of methodologies. Several of these contain trademarks or service marks. A list of these follows: Anat Baniel Method©, Bal-a-Vis-X™, Brain Gym®, Masgutova Neurosensorimotor Reflex Integration Method (MNRI®), TheraBand ™™™, Rhythmic Movement Training™

FIRST EDITION

Designed by Gessert Books

ISBN 978-0-9982480-0-4

Contents

Preface

Halfway through a presentation about learning differences, the mom next to me sighed and said, "Everything was fine until kindergarten!" Several other parents heard her and chuckled, as we all paused to remember. Our children had sparkled and dazzled us throughout their early years. But after kindergarten started, we began to hear reports from teachers: trouble sitting, problems using scissors, slow to read, messy handwriting. It seemed as though someone had changed the rules for success. And our children began to look weighed down by pressure.

Even though experts now report that there are ways to diagnose many learning differences (LDs) by age four, many children often don't get diagnosed until third grade or later. During this "don't know what's wrong" time, many teachers and parents just look at behavior. "Why isn't my child doing what he is supposed to?" "Is my child lazy?" "Am I parenting wrong?" Parents are often plagued with worries. And far too many children go to school every day with a sinking feeling of failure.

Once a teacher or parent identifies that a child is having trouble learning, that child can be diagnosed for an LD. If you're in the middle of this process, identifying the problem can seem like the most important step, but a diagnosis is only the beginning. After a diagnosis, it's time to make sure that your child is supported so that he can learn. And that can be the most difficult thing of all.

We used to assume schools would handle all learning needs. But if you listen to the harrowing stories of people who grew up with learning differences, LD children were often ridiculed or bullied, and many slipped through the cracks. Although our children's teachers are talented and work hard, many teachers still aren't taught how to identify or teach children who learn differently. Today's school system brings many new challenges: children must master academics at earlier ages; more time is spent on testing, school budgets have been slashed, and Common Core standards have changed how we teach and test.

In the shifting landscape of school, who is responsible for making sure their child succeeds? The parent. And supporting children with LDs has a steep learning curve.

It can be challenging for a parent to step in and try to help their LD child succeed in grammar school. This book will help. Written by a parent, and including many information sources, as well as hard-earned wisdom from hundreds of other parents, this book explains how you can successfully navigate the system for your child.

As parents, we want our children to succeed even if they think and learn differently. How can we help make this happen? With this book, you can start helping your child today.

CHAPTER 1:
When Your Child Has a Learning Difference

We should spend less time ranking children and more time helping them to identify their natural competencies and gifts and cultivate these. There are hundreds and hundreds of ways to succeed and many, many different abilities that will help you get there.

—*Dr. Howard Gardner, Frames of Mind*

Discovering that your child has a learning difference can shake your world. It's scary to hear from a teacher that your child has trouble learning, and painful when your child can't master academic skills the other kids are breezing through. After all, learning should be easy, right?

Although statistics for success are much higher when a child's learning differences (also called LDs) are discovered, diagnosed, and addressed in the early grades,[1] this success doesn't happen automatically. It can take years to identify and begin to help children with LDs. Parents report feeling overwhelmed and confused as they try to get help for their child.

In a situation where parents are often drowning in internet-search information, it's hard to find grounded advice on what to do, what to prioritize, and how to be effective. What can we say to a teacher to get help for our child in the classroom? What should we ask for? How can we help our child find success?

This book is written by a parent, for parents. It's based on years of research, interviews with experts, and advice from hundreds of parents, collected throughout the years. It contains a concise overview of the LD world, both at home and at school. It gives you information that will help you make better-informed decisions about how to help your child.

In particular, the early years of grammar school are very difficult for LD children and their families. Many parents have walked this road before you and have helped their children find success. You can do this, and your child can, too. We've been there. We know.

How Did This Book Start?

When my husband and I realized that our child was having unexpected and puzzling trouble in school, I spent a lot of time looking for a single professional who could guide us. We figured that there had to be a "learning doctor" who could tell us what to do, but we never found one. Instead, we found ourselves juggling many tasks:

- Nightly homework challenges with a distressed child
- Finding someone who could diagnose LDs
- Asking teachers and administrators for help
- Trying to understand how the school system offered support, and what the law says
- Learning about an entire world of diagnoses, specialists, insurance, and treatments

We were filled with questions. We knew nothing about brain development or LDs. We had no idea what the words meant, what the professionals did, what the tests measured, or even where to start.

As we spoke with and hired various professionals, not one of them was able to give us a top-down view of the LD landscape. Often, the professionals seemed to work in separate silos, not knowing or working with one another. And none of them talked with the teacher! We eventually learned that we had to do that research and put the pieces together. It was our job to make this work. Nobody was going to do it for us.

Our experience is one shared by countless parents. When you discover that your child has an LD, the subsequent testing, diagnosis, and educational needs are all unique. And trying to understand your child's problems, how he or she should be educated, and the inner workings of the educational and legal systems that educate and provide support can be overwhelming.

It's easy to feel isolated in the world of LD. After all, so many things apply just to your child. Abilities, challenges, needs, interests... But it turns out that many parents share your experience and can give valuable perspective and advice on the process of getting help and raising an LD child.

This book is the guide that we needed when we started. I hope that it helps you.

Is This Book for You?

Is your child having trouble in school? Is it difficult for your child to learn or remember things? Do you see a difference in performance between home and school? Are you spending hours on homework that should take 15 minutes? The symptoms go on and on.

Does your child forget things 10 minutes after you have taught her? Does she have meltdowns when she has to read or do homework? Is her handwriting illegible? Does he have trouble socializing? If you ask him to do three things at once, can he remember them all and complete the tasks? And are you re-teaching school every night, because your child doesn't seem to have learned anything during the school day?

Every one of those things is a sign that your child might have an LD. And there are more symptoms listed in Appendix B, "Symptoms of a Learning Difference."

If your child is having trouble fitting into school and learning, it will take some work to get appropriate identification, testing, and support. This book lays out a path you can follow. Although this book is written for parents of LD children who are in Kindergarten and grammar school, any parent can read it to get perspective and an overview.

This book doesn't focus on the needs of parents who have severe behavioral or psychological concerns about their children. It also is not meant in any way as a substitute for consulting a doctor.

Coming to Terms with an LD

Many articles talk about how distressing it is to discover that your child has an LD, and they often encourage parents to pass through all of the stages of grieving: denial, anger, bargaining, depression, and acceptance.

Don't grieve too soon, because identification, and even diagnosis, aren't the full story. Your child can do far better than the picture many professionals will paint. Many school problems are tied to brain maturity and children with LDs are often slow to mature, emotionally and intellectually. In the younger grades, children are not equipped to think their way around situations. Unexpected failure is hard to deal with as an adult. Imagine what it feels like to a child!

Young LD children often lack self-control, self-knowledge, ability to use tools that can help, and the ability to communicate their educational needs to teachers. All of these skills are learned as a child grows.

As this book will show, basic skills can be the most difficult for people who learn differently, but the world has changed. We all now carry around a tool in our pockets that can take pictures of white boards, take dictation, mail reminders, do calculations, and simplify our lives in many ways. Why not use it? New apps and tools are developed every day that can help people achieve. Targeted education, tools for learning, and schooling that identifies and teaches to strengths can help your child today.

At this point, most parents only know that the school is having trouble teaching their child, using the current techniques. Schools teach to one type of brain. LD children child have a different type. The experts who advise you on the status of your second grader don't have the hands-on wisdom that comes from parenting that same child through the years, and watching him find and apply his strengths in the world.

Moving forward, you might need to run interference with the school so that your child can succeed, and you'll need to learn more about what type of support your child needs to grow and learn. Children with LDs are often very bright and can do amazing things, so in the long run, "different" can have benefits.

Your child's future is open. It will take work to get there, but right now, you have no idea how far he can go.

Difference or Disability?

As you research LD issues, you'll notice that people in the medical and educational professions often use the term *learning disability* for a wide category of learning types and disorders.

In this book, we join a growing group of experts and parents who use the term *learning differences*. It's become clear that there are successful people with all different types of brains,[2] and experts are reporting that not only do LD brains work, but that many of them have measurable strengths, and sometimes those strengths are actually tied to their differences.[3]

If a child has a learning difference that qualifies for support in the school system, parents must invoke, learn, and understand federal laws in order to claim support. When they claim legal support, the parent uses the term *learning disability*.

That's because the laws that support equal access to education for children who learn differently are extensions of the IDEA (Individuals with Disability Education Act), and Section 504 of the Rehabilitation Act of 1973. IDEA is a powerful civil rights act that guarantees access to learning and Section 504 ensures equal access to education for children with LD. We describe support programs in Chapter 6, "School Support Programs for LD," and explain how to claim school support in Chapter 5, "Claiming School Support."

Regardless of the words that we need to use to get support from the school, parents can choose to have their own mindset and approach. Rather than telling their children they are disabled, many parents choose to teach their children that they learn differently.

As John, the father of a boy with LD says: "I don't want to parent from the perspective of limitations. I want to raise my child with a spirit of possibility. My son may need a different route, but there's nowhere he can't go."

What's a Learning Difference?

A "learning difference" means that it's somehow difficult for your child to learn and thrive in a typical school setting. Children with LDs usually have an intelligence level that's normal or higher than average, but they have a problem in one or more areas of learning because they see, hear, or understand things differently.[4]

We see LDs at every socioeconomic level. They are seen in all types of people, no matter how bright, and they're not caused by parenting.[5]

Learning differences are neurobiological[6]. People with LDs learn differently because of how their brains grow or function. And how children are educated has a big part in defining what makes an LD.

When a child has an LD, most often they have differences with how their brain:

- Receives input or processes information,
- Stores and retrieves information,
- Gets information out to the world, or
- Focuses and pays attention.

For more information on children's brains and LD, see Chapter 7, "What They Don't Tell You About Learning Differences."

A Surprising Number of Children Have Brains that Learn Differently

In 2015, 54.8 million students attended America's public elementary and secondary schools. [7] From 8 to 15% of children have an LD, [8] often undiagnosed.[9]

These are the most frequently diagnosed LDs:

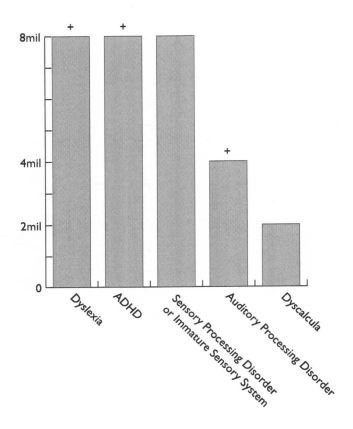

Many LDs overlap. About 50% of people with one LD will be diagnosed with one or more additional disorders,[10] Up to 14% of children who are identified as intellectually gifted may also have an LD.[11]

In 2014, 6.5 million children, aged 3 to 21, received special education services.[12] 35% of those students were diagnosed with *specific learning disabilities,*[13] such as the LDs we talk about in this book.

That's a lot of kids whose brains are not set up to automatically succeed in our school system.

The Most Common LDs

These LDs are explained more in Appendix A, "What's Inside Your Child's Diagnosis." [14]

Name of LD	Challenge	Example Problems in School
Dyslexia	Reading	Problems reading, writing, spelling, speaking, fine motor, memorizing, understanding time, and focus
Dysgraphia	Handwriting and written word organization	Hard to write, make letters, stay on line, and space letters. Often prints. Hard to organize ideas and spell.
Dyscalculia	Math	Problems with symbols, number sense, math problems, time, and money
Auditory Processing Disorder	Understanding speech, and responding	Language, reading, comprehension, memory.
ADHD	Attention	Problems focusing, and with impulsiveness, hyperactivity, or inattentiveness. Problems with self-motivation and control.

Other Conditions that Make Learning Difficult:

- **Memory problems**—Can affect either long-term or short-term (working) memory. Children with working memory problems have trouble holding a question in their brain while turning a page or looking for answers. Sometimes they learn, then immediately forget. Memory problems make it hard to memorize and retain even the simplest information, such as months, days of the week, birthday, telephone numbers, faces, letters. In their book, *The Mislabeled Child*, Dr. Brock and Dr. Fernette Eide explain the different types of working memory.

- **Sensory Processing Disorder or Immature Sensory System**—Problems standing, sitting, hearing, seeing, balance, and body sense. Child can be bothered by sound, visual input, and by clothing, and ordinary activities, such as bathing and hair-combing. Children may have problems with emotional regulation, difficulty focusing, and trouble performing academic skills.

- **Processing problems**—Can affect visual, auditory, language, and/or memory processing. Processing problems can affect a child's ability to accept input into the brain, understand it, act upon it, or produce output. Can affect reasoning, making it hard to multi-task, and causing the child to respond and work slowly. If a child has multiple types of processing problems, it can be difficult to use input to solve a problem and then write down the solution.

- **Executive Function**—Can affect organization, setting up goals, and getting things done. Includes trouble organizing thought and action and solving problems. Problems starting, sticking with, and finishing tasks.

- **Social Skills**—Many children (up to 75% of students with LD[15]) have a hard time intuitively understanding the rules around social skills Their problems include understanding how to connect with others, poor communication skills, and defensiveness.

- **Just Being Different**—Some children are slow to mature, have brain areas that mature at different speeds, or their brains just work differently. This can include very gifted children, who often develop in individual fashions.

If You Hear "Lazy," Think LD

If your child is having trouble in school, the teacher can interpret it in two ways. One way is to blame the child (often noting that the child is lazy, or doesn't do their work), and another way is to flag and respond to a possible LD.

Children, especially young children, generally want to have accomplishments and please their parents and teachers.[16] If your child has great behavior at home, but you keep getting reports from a teacher that they are lazy or deliberately won't do their work at school, it's good policy to take a closer look. Other first indicators of an LD are:

- Avoids or is slow to learn letters, reading, or writing,

- Very sloppy work,
- Has a very hard time with homework.

LDs can affect perception, processing, or the ability to produce schoolwork. They can also affect memory, focus, and the ability to organize. Auditory processing problems can look like focus problems, and focus problems can look like a bad attitude.

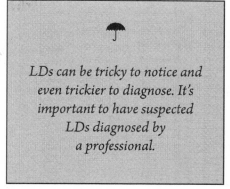

LDs can be tricky to notice and even trickier to diagnose. It's important to have suspected LDs diagnosed by a professional.

Appendix B describes more LD symptoms. For information about getting your child tested and getting support for your child in school, see Chapter 5, "Claiming Support in the School System." If you decide to have your child tested by a professional outside of the school, Appendix D, "Types of Doctors and Specialists," lists doctors who test for LD.

Many LDs Share Common Problems

It turns out that children with LDs share many common characteristics: problems and strengths alike. Unfortunately, very few parents know about these common problems.

Sharon, the mother of a boy with several LDs, says "When I visited a dyslexia school, after five years of helping my son with LD, I mentioned to the admissions counselor that my son was bright but had problems with memorizing multiplication, and even knowing the months of the year. The counselor laughed. "Oh, all of our kids have that," she said. She then explained that it's extremely common for dyslexic or other LD students to have a whole group of problems."

Sharon is still amazed. "To this day, I don't understand why educators and professionals don't tell parents right away to expect these troubles, and to work around them. We spent three full summers time memorizing multiplication tables, only to have him forget them two weeks later. I had no idea why he couldn't memorize. I was so scared!"

It's also very common for children with LDs to be late bloomers, and to have a brain that develops unevenly.[17] Almost every LD child eventually develops basic skills, but in a timeframe that lags behind their peers, often up to several years. Shared problems include:

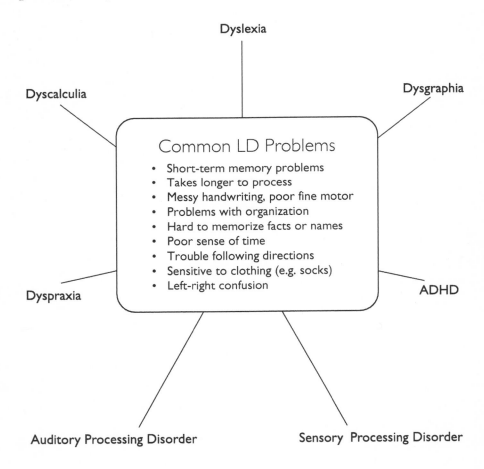

Dyslexia

Dyscalculia

Dysgraphia

Common LD Problems

- Short-term memory problems
- Takes longer to process
- Messy handwriting, poor fine motor
- Problems with organization
- Hard to memorize facts or names
- Poor sense of time
- Trouble following directions
- Sensitive to clothing (e.g. socks)
- Left-right confusion

Dyspraxia

ADHD

Auditory Processing Disorder

Sensory Processing Disorder

LD children should not be punished for these, or other challenges. Often, parents need to work with the teacher to get *accommodations* because certain actions aren't yet neurologically possible. We can certainly learn from Sharon, though. Her son eventually learned to multiply in 8th grade. Chapter 4, "Helping Your Child Succeed in School," talks about accommodations.

We Now Know That LDs Also Have Associated Strengths

It's a natural step to identify your LD child's challenges. But it's not always such a natural step to identify her strengths. Many books and articles encourage parents to identify their children's strengths, but many parents have no idea of what those strengths look like. "It felt like all of the other kids were playing violin or were soccer stars," said Brenda. "Was there some gift that was supposed to develop all of a sudden?"

Many people and organizations through the years have written and spoken out about the gifts and strengths of people who learn differently. This includes Linda Silverman, Ph.D., who wrote the book *Upside-Down Brilliance: The Visual-Spatial Learner*, Dr. Hallowell, who wrote *Superparenting for ADD*, and Dr. Fernette Eide and Dr. Brock Eide, authors of *The Dyslexic Advantage: Unlocking the Hidden Potential of the Dyslexic Brain*, and creators of the Dyslexic Advantage online community at www.dyslexicadvantage.com.

Many of these particular strengths won't become apparent until your child is considerably older. If you have a young child, and you don't see strengths that you recognize on this list, don't worry. It's a myth that every child displays a specific "gift" at a young age. It's fine to just be a child who demonstrates good qualities, like a good sense of humor, sense of fun, and the ability to ask for and give help. Chapter 3, "Your Journey," describes more valuable qualities that contribute to success.

Children develop in surprising and amazing ways, but it takes time. Many parents of older students who were worried about their children in early grades now report that their children have many of the strengths mentioned in this diagram[18], and more.

Strengths and Abilities Associated with Learning Differences

Determination

- Hard working
- Resilient
- Driven to achieve
- Persistent
- Enthusiastic
- High Integrity
- Gets things done

Information Skills

- Recognizes patterns in information
- Creates internal pictures of complex situations
- "Just knows" the answer, but can't explain why
- Holistic way of viewing information/tasks to do
- Strong visual-spatial skills
- Strong auditory skills
- Strong verbal skills

Creative Skills

- Great at building or creating
- Artistic
- Musical
- Spontaneous
- Unique viewpoint
- Strong sense of humor

People Skills

- Empathetic
- Caring
- Open and aware
- Generous
- Leadership
- Management skills

Thinking Skills

- Curious
- Absorbs information from several sources at the same time
- Connects many different concepts
- Can see relationships between ideas and concepts that others miss
- Good at problem-solving
- Can see the big picture
- Develops new knowledge, instead of just memorizing existing knowledge
- Strong memory ability, such as narrative, color, emotional, visual, or sensory
- Uses unique or personal associations to aid memory

Children with LDs Can and Do Succeed

It's very difficult to have an LD, and it requires a lot of work. But as children develop, their ability to learn changes. Support, coupled with early remedial learning and/or therapies can have life-changing effects on LDs.

Some behaviors treated as weaknesses in school turn out to be strengths in the dynamic business world. There are many stories of LD children growing up to become CEOs, inventors, adventurers, teachers, actors, and people who make a difference in the world. Several books have been written, analyzing different thought patterns of dyslexics, and why they can bring value.[19] A recent study reports that 38% of entrepreneurs are dyslexic,[20] and many entrepreneurs talk about having ADHD.

Here are just a few of the successful people who have talked about having LDs.

LD	*Who Has This LD?*
Dyslexia (reading)	Richard Branson, Charles Schwab, Jamie Oliver, Kiera Knightley, Tim Tebow, Anderson Cooper
Dysgraphia (handwriting)	Agatha Christie, Albert Einstein, George Patton, Liv Tyler
ADHD	Justin Timberlake, Michael Phelps, Simone Biles
Dyspraxia (motor skills)	Daniel Radcliffe, Cara Delevingne
Apraxia (motor speech)	Ronda Rousey
Dyscalculia (math)	Henry Winkler, Thomas Edison (possibly)

In interviews, many of these people have said their LD challenges in grammar and middle school years were far more challenging than in their adult lives, where they could work around issues.

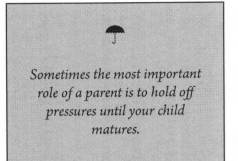

Sometimes the most important role of a parent is to hold off pressures until your child matures.

As you look around your own life, realize that many of the people you know and work with have some sort of LD—but you probably can't tell. To the parent of a child who is coping with what looks like endless failures in the school system, the pressures are intense. It's very important to realize that your neighbor has dyslexia, and the man across the hall has to use a calculator to do math.

If you are a parent looking at your young child in the school system and feeling overwhelmed, realize that educational tests only measure your child's status today—they don't predict the future. Your child will grow, strengthen, and blossom. Things will get better with maturity and support.

How to Use This Book

Children grow in stages, and you'll support your LD child through many years of school. Think of this book as a guidebook for that journey.

As we raise a child, we're responsive to social pressures. We want our child to be polite, to not have screaming tantrums in the market, and to not litter. It's easy to get anxious if it feels like our child isn't doing the correct thing. When our child has learning problems, it can feel embarrassing if our child isn't doing homework, or is failing tests. How do we handle this?

Children with LD can be judged harshly in school, so parents must remain vigilant, especially for younger LD children who haven't learned to advocate for themselves. Chapter 2, "Protect," contains wisdom from parents of older children. It talks about how to actively protect your child during this time of stress, and Chapter 2 talks about how to work with the school, and how to deal with difficult situations that may arise.

Chapter 3, "Your Journey," discusses how *you* will change as you pass through this experience. These are the types of lessons that parents look back and think "I wish I would have known this when I started." Learning how to deal with professionals, interview specialists and interact successfully with your child's school are big, powerful skills. You'll learn and exercise abilities that will travel with you throughout your life, like trusting yourself, being clear about what you want —moving on if you don't get it—and speaking up if something isn't right. You'll come through this journey with some amazing abilities and achievements.

Three of the chapters in this book deal with the school system. Chapter 4, "Helping Your Child Succeed in School," talks about the basics: how to partner effectively with your child's teacher, how to manage and present information, and what you need to know about teaching and accommodations for an LD child.

If you suspect an LD, it's best to take advantage of school-supplied LD testing, and claim support. Chapter 5, "Claiming Support in the School System" explains how to do this, by walking you through a simplified version of the process and explaining how to claim support and disagree with the school system, if necessary.

Chapter 6, "School Support Programs for LD," describes the types of school programs available to your child. It explains each one, and describes benefits and disadvantages.

Chapter 7, "What They Don't Tell You About Learning Differences," explains how LDs are diagnosed, and why it's sometimes difficult to determine exactly which LD/s your child has. It also explains how to look inside of your child's diagnosis, and describes how therapy can help with maturity and performance.

Many books are thick and overwhelming. I've kept this book short on purpose—so that you can quickly come up to speed. In order to do this, I've taken some of the "listy stuff" and put it into Appendices.

Appendix A, "What's Inside Your Child's Diagnosis?" allows you to look under the umbrella of most popular diagnoses by listing typical weaknesses found in each diagnosis. You can use this list when you go over your child's test results and talk with her doctor. It can help you determine how you will support your child's learning, and help you develop priorities.

Appendix A also contains a glossary of terms that might be new to you.

Appendix B, "Symptoms of a Learning Difference," contains an overview of symptoms that could indicate a LD.

Appendix C, "The Whole-Child Diagnostic Approach," describes what other parents have tested in their efforts to identify factors that affect focus and academic abilities.

Appendix D, "Types of Doctors and Specialists" describes the different types of specialists that you might deal with, and talks about their qualifications, and whether or not they can diagnose LDs or ADHD. It also includes a list of professional organizations that can help you find specialists.

Appendix E, "Sample Letters," contains several samples of the types of letters that you will need to write in order to request support for your child.

The BrainParenting Book Series

This is the first book in the BrainParenting book series. BrainParenting books are short, direct, contain useful information, and will guide you as you help your child. *Fine Until Kindergarten: A Parent's First Guide to Learning Differences* is an overview book for every parent of an LD child.

To join the email list for upcoming books, go to www.fineuntilkindergarten.com and sign up for our reader's list.

Throughout this book, you'll see links to reference material. In the paper version of this book, we include the entire URL, so you can also go to our website at www.fineuntilkindergarten.com/Bonus to see references and bonus reference material on one clickable page.

18

CHAPTER 2:
Protect Your Child

It's time to reject the model that emphasizes what's wrong, disabled, disordered, and diseased, and replace it with a model that emphasizes what's right, what's good, what's strong… Instead of feeling like a disabled child, in need of treatment, the child can feel like a champion in the making.

—*Dr. Edward Hallowell, Their Brilliant Minds*

We spend all of childhood protecting our children. We protect them from the elements, other children, from cliffs, treetops, and dangerous snakes, but what happens when they enter school and have problems? Often, that protection wavers, as parents spend time wondering why their LD child isn't doing what he's supposed to. Teachers don't always have time or training to understand why a child under-performs, and some have been known to take it personally if a child does poor-quality work.

Although the path of childhood is traditionally well-protected, there is no automatic safe zone for a child with LDs. This leaves children with LDs unprotected from failure, a sense of worthlessness, and from teaching strategies that don't help them learn. As parents, we need to make sure that our children are supported as they learn.

Relentless Failure is Bad for Children

What happens when a child goes to school every single day and fails? This is a common pattern for a child with an LD. Relentless failure can eat away at self-esteem, and many children with LDs call themselves "stupid." Self-limiting beliefs can harm a child's future. Both scientific evidence and our own eyes tell us that a panicked, despondent child's brain is shut down and cannot learn.[21]

We've all heard the stories about that one wonderful teacher whose kind words spurred someone on to conquer the world. But what about the teacher who humiliates a child, mocks their work in public, doesn't follow an IEP or 504 plan[22] because they don't "believe" in it, gives "F's" to a child instead of changing teaching methods, and treats an LD child like a loser? Exposure to teachers who aren't supportive and who don't teach in a way that lets LD children learn can be a real part of many of our children's lives.

Painful classroom and teacher experiences don't just fade away. Studies of dyslexic students have shown that negative experiences can have a life-long impact on self-esteem[23]—and poor self-esteem often leads to poor choices in life.[24] Some parents report feeling like their child's spirit was being slowly crushed in a bad school situation.

Your Child's School Experience

In general, parents are not taught to be wary of what school does to our children. That's considered irrational and overprotective. In some cases, it *is* overprotective. In other cases, it's a way to verify that our child's needs are being met.

Teachers: Trust but Verify

Teachers represent infinite possibility and resources to our children. However, many children taken out of school by a parent had a negative experience with a teacher who was not trained to identify and/or support that child's LDs, either in the techniques that she used, or in the approach that she brought to the table. And in many cases, the school districts also didn't offer support. It's a delicate situation, here's some advice:

- Do let your child's teacher teach. Train your children to respect the position of teacher. Teachers spend all day, every day surrounded by up to 30 children, and represent vast amounts of knowledge. A good teacher will have a whole bag of tricks that she can use—many different ways to present information so that a child can "see" it and can understand and learn it.

- As part of normal development, every child needs to step away from her parents and go into a classroom where the rules are set down and enforced by a totally different individual: the teacher. Learning to follow rules, to get along with, and to trust teachers is an important developmental step.

- Manage your teacher relationship. Educate yourself and monitor your child's status in the classroom, and don't be afraid to get involved (always keeping emotions calm and asking for clarification first). You're in partnership with this teacher.

Flipping the Fail-First Approach

A surprising amount of school is based upon a "fail first" approach.[25] Children are tested to see where they're weak, then taught to fill the holes. Children are watched to see if they misbehave, and if they do, they receive consequences.

Although experts agree that school failure should not be how we identify children with LD,[26] it is still the standard operating procedure in most schools. And because their school experience is defined negatively, many LD children consider themselves failures.

21

Because LD children already have low self-esteem, continued fail-first approaches, or a teacher who punishes them for learning differently, can lead to depression, lack of trying, and sometimes even poor behavior.

Studies show that positive teaching techniques are most effective for teaching LD children. Studies also show that smaller class size, early identification, more teacher training, and improved instruction can help LD children to succeed, but these aren't yet available in every school system.[27] In the meantime, the parent is left to smooth a path for their child.

It's important to protect your child from punishment and humiliation because of an LD.

- Make sure that your child's teacher understands that your child's brain works differently. Bring literature. Have a talk. In many cases, teachers have never heard of specific LDs and haven't been educated in LD teaching techniques. Sometimes, teachers don't understand why accommodations are necessary. You'll need to diplomatically educate the teacher and often, the school.

- Especially if it's tied to academic performance, ask the the teacher to not send home any "red cards," or flags that call attention to your child's performance problems.

- Ask the teacher not to mark how many problems your child gets wrong on a test. Write what he gets *correct*, instead.

- If you see a pattern of teaching that is affecting your child negatively, talk with the teacher. Suggest alternatives.

- Work with the teacher to place your child into situations where it is possible for him to succeed, by identifying interests, opportunities, strengths, and by using accommodations.[28]

- At home, work with your child to set one or more goals, and then work toward them. Help your child learn what types of effort will meet his goals. These goals can be non-academic. Perhaps learning a sport or a skill, or creating a project, saving money for, or collecting items. The process of setting goals, then fulfilling them

through real effort is one of the most powerful
self-esteem boosters.

- Watch your criticism. Your child is in a situation where he receives criticism every single day. Try to balance things out. One way is to look for three positive (real) things your child does every day, and comment on them. Specialists encourage parents to use positive, specific terms when complementing, and to complement hard work, as opposed to "smartness."[29]

- Give your child breaks. Have some fun together.

Dealing with Rough Situations

Every schoolchild has troubles at school sometimes. Most of those situations are to be expected and can be dealt with normally. However, sometimes a bad situation will arise that needs special involvement. For example:

- Your child is showing misery, or strong stress or anxiety.
- Your child cannot keep up with the school and homework load.
- Your teacher isn't following accommodations.
- Your child is being bullied.

Your child's mental health is top priority. Misery doesn't strengthen children and can do real damage. If your child is in crisis, parents advise that you do what you need to do, even if you need to remove your child from school for a few days. (Make sure that you're familiar with your school district's rules. Some districts enforce truancy. In that case, you might be able to work with your doctor and take a medical break due to anxiety.) You can continue negotiating and talking with the school even if your child is taking a short break.

Homework Stress

Many children with LDs have homework stress every night. If you compare a child with LDs with a classmate, you'll see that even a simple homework assignment—no big deal to a classmate—can be stressful and difficult for the LD child. Some parents report that their children cry every night before they even try to do homework, and other parents report that homework takes hours every night—even in lower grades.

In homework stress situations, it's important to pull back and look at the bigger picture. How are you handling homework?

Our culture often expects that parents help their children with homework. Many of us end up sitting with our children every night doing homework, until we start to almost fight their homework battle ourselves. Three big things to remember:

- *The parent should not be re-teaching school every night.* If you are doing this, pull back. Your teacher shouldn't send homework home that your child cannot do. If your child doesn't know how to do her homework, the school is failing her, and you need to meet with the teacher and work to set up an alternate strategy.

- *In the lower grades, your child probably shouldn't have more than 15 or 20 minutes of homework a night*[30]. The National Education Foundation recommends 10-20 minutes per night in first grade, and an additional 10 minutes a night for each subsequent grade.[31] Studies show that children with LDs in particular should get simple, short homework assignments.[32]

- *Don't work at a student level. Work at an executive level.* If your child's teacher is assigning too much work, *do not* overdo it every night, trying to keep up. Set up a meeting with her as soon as possible, and reduce your child's homework load.

Children with LD often have learning needs that are not met by homework. [33] If your child needs to do *occupational therapy* or another therapy to stimulate motor skills or brain development, go ahead and schedule it in. If your child is doing work with a tutor, it's sometimes less effective to do homework than focus on missing or weak skills. (See also "Working With Professionals," in Chapter 3, "Your Journey.") In both of these cases, it's perfectly all right to talk with the teacher about reducing homework. In a few lucky cases, parents have tutors talk with teachers so the two can partner up.

Homework troubles are one of the reasons why parents formally request an *IEP evaluation*. If your child is tested and qualifies, the school must, by law, set up an *independent educational plan* (IEP). Other children qualify for 504 plans. For more information on types of support that you can claim, see Chapter 6, "School Support Programs for LD."

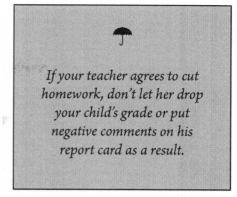

If your teacher agrees to cut homework, don't let her drop your child's grade or put negative comments on his report card as a result.

Chapter 5, "Claiming Support the School System," describes how to claim support.

Making a Difficult Teacher Situation Work

Most parents report dealing with several teachers who just didn't "click," or who taught in a way that didn't work for their children. Parents are taught that our children need to learn how to get along with different types of teachers, and that's true. But if a child has LDs, is socially unskilled, or if he has ADHD, in which children are said to have a maturity level of up to three years younger than their physical age,[34] having a supportive teacher is important, especially in the younger grades.

If your child is beginning to show stress in a classroom, go ahead and meet with the teacher. Get to know how the teacher works. Does she have any ideas for how to support your non-standard learner? Will she work with your child in a positive way? Is she comfortable working with accommodations?

If you find yourself repeatedly working to intercede on your child's behalf across the board, especially for the same things, consider that this might not be the correct teacher for your child. In that case, write the issues down to summarize them, and meet with your principal to ask for help. (Chapter 4, "Helping Your Child Succeed in School," explains more about keeping and using information.)

Managing teacher relationships can be very difficult, because sometimes you have to criticize a professional, and that can be touchy business. Here some general tips to help:

- Stay diplomatic: pleasant and professional. Teaching is very hard work and deserves respect.

- You and the teacher are on the same side. It's good to mention that, and approach any conversation with that in mind.

- Be careful with your language. Don't accuse or condemn. Ask questions. Ask the teacher for ideas and suggestions.

- If your child has come home and reported something, when you then meet with the teacher you can ask the teacher for a description of the event. Don't tell the teacher what your child said and expect her to respond to it.

- Respect the fact that your teacher may have an entire system for managing your child's needs that you don't know about. Be there to learn. And also, respect that your child's needs may require the teacher to grow many new skills. Be tactful.

- Create a paper trail as described in Chapter 4. Summarize results of a meeting and send it to the teacher nicely, as "my understanding." If you need to act, the paper trail will be your justification.

- Show up with a coffee, and perhaps a roll. Be friendly.

Try everything you can first. Moving classrooms is hard and should be avoided if possible. But if the experience of being in this teacher's class is causing your child real trauma, move heaven and earth to get your child in with a more supportive teacher.

If you decide that a move is necessary, lay out the situation for the principal, show your evidence, and ask clearly and directly for your child to be moved. Tell the principal where you want your child moved, if possible, and keep following up.

Bullying

More than 45% of parents of LD children report that their child has been bullied.[35] Studies show that children struggling with LDs may be more likely to be bullied or ostracized.[36] It's important to have a zero tolerance for bullying and traumatizing of your child. And your children, like all children, should be taught to not tolerate bullying.

If you suspect bullying, you should bring it up immediately with your child, and with the teacher and school. There are laws and resources designed to protect children with LDs against bullying,[37] and many schools have anti-bullying programs. If your child reports that he has been bullied:

- Listen to what your child says and believe her if she tells you about a bullying situation. Let your child know that you support her, that bullying is not her fault, and that it is unacceptable. Ask for details.

- If your child has trouble in social situations, make sure that she is really experiencing targeted bullying, and that she isn't misunderstanding rudeness, meanness, and bullying.[38] Appendix C, "Types of Doctors and Specialists," lists specialists who can help with social skills.

- Don't let your emotions guide you. Be effective. Don't retaliate. You are modeling behavior for your child. Show her how to handle this.

- If your child is experiencing physical danger or harm, remove her from the situation.

- Talk with the teacher and ask about her observations. Then ask for suggestions. You can also talk with the counselor. If the bullying is extreme, go right to the principal.

- Write down everything that happens, the dates, and who is involved. Send follow-up emails with goals. Save your notes in your records. If the school has a written policy on bullying, get a copy and include it in your records.

- Coach your child on how to react, if possible. Help her name what's going on by calling it "bullying," and encourage her to speak out and loudly say "Stop it!"

- Give it a week. If the bullying continues, visit the principal, give him a written summary from your notes, ask what the school can do to keep your child safe. Get support for yourself, and keep pushing.

As you deal with the situation, make sure that you go out of the way to expose your child to something positive—an after-school sport or friendship that will let her experience a positive experience at this time.

At the same time as you deal with administration, look around to see if there are allies who can help your child during the day. Talk with her teachers, counselor, the yard duty people, the librarian. Who is near when the bullying is happening? Educate them on the situation and formulate a plan. Sometimes letting your child know that there's a safe place near means that she can escape from difficult situations while you're working out a plan at the administrative level.

Are there friendly children? Sometimes it helps to talk with friendly parents, or parents of friendly children and formulate strategies to use during the day. Bullying, after all, is a problem with the system, and everyone should want to eradicate it. Sometimes, parents have pressured administration to bring in external bullying presentations. Other times, parents have taken turns volunteering on the school yard during lunch time. You can also visit the school to observe.

An excellent organization for bullying advice is Pacer (www.pacer.org.) If you need to contact an advocacy organization, Pacer suggests visiting ParentCenterNetwork.org or calling 888.248-0822.

Beyond the Principal

If you take a situation to the principal and are unhappy with his action, you can send a brief email describing the situation and requesting a meeting to the school superintendent, copying the principal, special education director, and chair of the school board. Print out a copy of the letter for your records. Keep following up (and documenting your efforts) until you get response.

If your child has been granted educational support for a learning disability with an Independent Educational Plan (IEP), your child is protected by law. The IDEA law provides a process for solving problems, as described in Chapter 5.

The Power and Danger of Labels

When we diagnose and treat these kids we often, inadvertently, instill the most dangerous learning disabilities... what truly holds people back in life. The dangerous disabilities are fear, shame, loss of hope... and a feeling of being less-than. Those are the disablers. Without meaning to, teachers, parents, doctors, and other professionals instill these disablers every day—in the name of helping children.

—Dr. Ed. Hallowell, *Their Beautiful Minds*

Labeling is not a casual thing. It has power.

Negative messages affect children. You will learn to speak out and actively advocate so your child will receive protection and support as he learns. Your child is watching. As you model advocacy behavior, he will learn to advocate for himself. Be careful and conscious about the words that you use, and the words that you teach him to use about himself.

Like many issues around raising a child who learns differently, there are no simple solutions. When you go to the school to negotiate support for your child, you will need to use the term "learning disability" to qualify for services. It might help you or your child to be specific about diagnostic terms at some other points in your child's life as well. (See also Chapter 4, "Helping Your Child Succeed in School.")

Some parents use the term "learning difference" and encourage their child to realize that everyone's brain is different, with unique strengths and weaknesses. Other parents feel that it empowers their child when they teach their child that they have a "learning disability" and that they should speak up and educate people about it.

Some parents actively reject the idea that their child is disabled, and work hard to find education that supports them as different learners. Many of these parents end up homeschooling their children, because they can use positive approaches that support their child's success, instead of emphasizing failures. You can choose what terms work best for your child and family.

Labels Can Affect Perception and Treatment

Make sure that you're comfortable with the terms that you use when you present your child to others. Try to choose a term that is effective, and make sure that you don't label your child in situations where it will make it harder for her.

- Be very careful using medical diagnostic terms outside of the classroom. LD terms can cause people to judge your child harshly. It's a good idea to always think about *why* you are describing your child. Do you want your child's behavior understood empathetically by a coach? Or are you explaining to a teacher why your child's LD affects classroom performance, so that she can craft a learning experience around it?

  If you're just watching out for your child in a social or sport situation, you can use terms like *shy, anxious, immature,* or *uncoordinated.* These real words aren't scary. For example, if your child is awkward socially or has left-right issues, it's best to tell a soccer coach that she has some anxiety, or gets confused about left and right, rather than using labeling terms like ADHD or dyslexia. A soccer coach isn't educated in LDs.

  Whenever possible choose an effective, positive way to describe your child. Compare:

My child is bad at math.	vs	My child has trouble visualizing math, and works best when you demonstrate with manipulatives.
My child can't sit still.	vs	My child focuses better when he moves his body.

On the left side is a simple statement, describing a child's failure or problem. On the right are alternate ways of communicating that information. Both examples offer a solution or reason for the behavior, giving the teacher or coach a way to help the child. Appendix A, "What's Inside Your Child's Diagnosis," lists which skills are typically weak within each diagnosis, and can help you be specific.

- Many people know nothing about LDs. Some people confuse autism, dyslexia, and ADHD, so if you mention one term, you can find yourself trying to explain how your child does NOT have the other two terms—which can cause even more confusion.

Eva, the mother of an LD child, once told a real estate agent that her child had dyslexia. "Will she be able to be with her own kind?" asked the agent, sympathetically.

- Many parents suggest that you try to keep the conversation less about what your child "has" and more about what your child "needs," in order to succeed.

- Some parents report that a low key "I learn differently" or "I use audio books for reading" works well, especially for young children.

Speaking about LDs in Front of Your Child

As Jenifer Fox says, in her book, *Your Child's Strengths*, "The language parents and teachers use with and in front of children is critical to developing strength or focusing on weakness."

One of the biggest things to remember when raising an LD child is to be very careful about what you say in front of your child—and make sure that others are as well. While your choices may be different, here are some suggestions:

- Don't discuss your child's issues with specialists in front of your child. Don't let specialists engage in labelling or pathologizing your child in front of your child.

- Don't let teachers issue critiques in front of your child. Listen to what the teacher says first, and if there are one or two messages that you want your child to hear, bring your child in once you know what the teacher is going to say.

- Put other descriptive words into your child's ears. Maybe she has a good sense of direction, or is great with animals. Perhaps he is great with children and a "born teacher," or an artist, or loves to cook. Your child should get practice defining himself in positive terms. Point out or spend time with adults with similar gifts, so your child can see adults like him.

Be Cautious of the Push to Self-label

Many people think that self-knowledge is the same thing as self-labeling. It is not. Knowledge brings power. Labeling can bring bad feelings if it's not done right.

Shelly's daughter was under a lot of stress and was starting to have some obsessions. Shelly found a workbook for children that talked about overcoming obsessive-compulsive disorder (OCD). "I thought the book would be great," said Shelly. "It used real words and I thought it would help my daughter identify a feeling, and build skills to help deal with it. So I ordered it, but when I got it, the entire book kept saying *You have OCD.* They used the label again and again. I just wanted to give her some coping techniques, not a psychiatric label. And I certainly didn't want her to start telling herself that she has a psychiatric condition just because she read a workbook."

It's a good idea to read help books before giving them to your child, and to watch out for messages that your child receives. How does your child refer to herself? Early self-labeling can internalize and stay with a child. Pay attention to words and messages and choose them consciously.

Some people want to use the term, "disability," from an early age. But if your child could succeed in a differently-structured learning environment, is she still disabled? First grade is not life. It's a specific learning situation.

How a Diagnosis Can Help

So if labeling isn't good for children, why diagnose children with LDs? Kids like to work, to achieve, to do well. And a lot of kids with LDs report feeling like they're "stupid," and "losers."

It turns out that if you help a child who is struggling in school figure out what's going on and why he learns differently, and then if you get help for him, and teach him how to "drive" his particular brain to success, it can be a life-changer.

Many adults with LDs talk of how relieved they were to discover that they had dyslexia, dyspraxia, auditory processing, or other problems. *It meant that they weren't stupid.* This can also be a good reason for sharing a diagnosis with your child. Not to label, but to explain, to lift the hood on his brain so he can understand it and operate it better.

As one parent pointed out, you can call the diagnosis whatever you want. Rick Riordan, author of the beloved "Lightening Thief" book series, conceived of the series after telling bedtime stories to his son, who has ADHD and dyslexia. In Rick's book series, ADHD and dyslexia are signs of being a half-blood, or demigod.

Studies that focus on success have found that perception is surprisingly powerful. If a person believes that they are in control of their lives and that effort and ability determine their future, they are measurably more successful than people who believe that luck, chance, or other people's behavior control their fate.[39]

Even if you have multiple diagnoses, what you call yourself can be important.

Protecting Your Family and Home Life

Today's world is a pressure cooker for both children and parents. In a situation where your child has an LD, the pressure to succeed at school can take over your life. Some of the best advice for LD parents comes from Russell Barkley, Ph.D., a renowned ADHD expert who encourages parents to develop "executive skills" in order to help their children.[40] In his book *Taking Charge of ADHD—The Complete Authoritative Guide for Parents*, Barkley describes skills that all LD parents could use: how to develop driving principles, how to manage your time, and how to use a scientific approach with your child: experimenting and revising.

Barkley also talks about keeping school performance in perspective. He talks about how easy it is to damage the child-parent bond by focusing too hard on achievement—and too little on who your child is. He also talks about how parents can set priorities. The priorities he mentions include:

Sense of Family—Make family and your family relationships a priority. Separate from school stress as often as possible, and don't make every communication with your child be about accomplishment. Tell stories about your parents, your grandparents, and how your family came to be where it is. What traits helped them? Push back on achievement pressure.

Honor time with all of your children, and work to create a shared life with solid underpinnings. Try playing some old-fashioned games. Do things together, like building a garden, or working on a volunteer project. Work is a great experience: it helps with bonding and creates self-esteem. Enjoy your family. In the middle of school pressures, we sometimes forget to take time for us.

Sense of Community—Belonging to a community is something that we all need, and your child may need real help in finding communities where he can belong. It's important for people to belong and feel connected.

Model community involvement. Reach out and include your child, and help her find organizations and communities where she can be appreciated and have fun. Look at community gardens, park cleanup days, or visiting seniors. Janelle reports that her son always enjoyed working or helping the community. "He found it much less stressful than having people watch him to see if he was having enough fun," she says.

Mental Health and Balance—Whether or not your child is diagnosed with ADHD, the ADHD books often discuss mental health and school struggles in the most direct, helpful fashion. We don't just raise our children to be physically healthy. We also raise them to learn how to help themselves and others, and deal with adversity. We develop mental health and balance through free time, recreation, hobbies, and informal sports. All of these should have a place in our child's world.

In his book, *Superparenting for ADD*, Dr. Edward Hallowell, talks about ways to deal with your child's challenges, and how to look for *mirror traits*, the positive traits inside of negative abilities or behavior. By looking at a child as having unwrapped potential strengths, you can help a child avoid shame and fear. For more information on developing success traits and life balance, see Chapter 3, "Your Journey."

Protecting Siblings—It can be hard for siblings of LD children. Often, the LD child gets far more attention, and many times, the family's finances (and sometimes vacation time) are spent supporting LD needs.

If you are seeing trouble between siblings, it might be a good idea to explain a little bit about LD, and what it means, says Betty Osman, Ph.D.[41] LD in the family is a life problem and it's a good idea to talk about challenges and how to approach them, and to model problem-solving for all siblings. Parents caution against making one sibling responsible for another, but if one child seems to attend more fun events, it might be a good idea to explain why.

If your children go to the same school, teachers often project performance from one sibling onto another. "Our LD son was the oldest child," said Laurie, mother of three. When his younger brother entered the classroom the following year, they had a chat with teachers. "We needed to reset their expectations, so they didn't treat the two brothers the same, said Laurie. "We just kept an eye on it."

Sense of Joy—At least occasionally, your family should experience less technology and more physical fun. As Lawrence Cohen, Ph.D. says, in his book *Playful Parenting*, "in order to be fountains of hopefulness and enthusiasm for our children, we must find ways to replenish ourselves." Sharing fun activities can help the entire family.

CHAPTER 3:
Your Journey

"If the path before you is clear, you're probably on someone else's."

—*Joseph Campbell*

As our children grow, we turn to our family, friends, and communities for advice on parenting issues. We ask the mom next to us at the park how she deals with teething. We ask our sister how she potty-trained. As a society, we share parenting tips, stories, and wisdom.

If your child has an LD, though, this easy sharing of experiences stops. You become the expert on your child — because LD issues are often specific and unique. Instead of gathering input from friends and family, you start staying up late, searching the internet for answers. You buy new parenting books with names like *The Challenging, Difficult, Complex, Never-Stopping, Ninja Child*, or *Multisensory Memorization*.

It can be frustrating, trying to figure out how to support your child's learning and empower her to succeed. Part of the journey is yours. You will learn new skills, and become an expert on your child and the school system. You will get a black belt in patience. This journey will take a lot of love and effort, but you can do it.

Forging Your Own Path

Wrangling a child with an LD through the educational system can be quite a journey. Although every LD child is unique, many challenges in the system are similar. In this chapter, we bring you advice and knowledge from parents and professionals that can help you meet the challenges. Some of the things you'll learn:

- A different perspective. Your child's successes might look very different from yours. Measure success and progress on his trajectory, not yours.

- You'll learn that some professionals "get" your child and some do not, and you can choose to work with those who do.

- You'll become an expert in your child's needs. And you'll discover that what works well for other children's needs might not help your child.

- You'll learn to resourcefully and diplomatically help shape your child's environment, so that it's possible to learn and succeed.

Attitudes Matter

We all know that children pay more attention to what we do than to what we say. They feel our attitudes and emotions. So our attitudes have a profound effect on how our children view themselves and approach difficulties.

As you parent your LD child, you'll find yourself re-thinking some ideas that you've taken for granted, especially about success and failure.

The Path to Success

We often pick up a definition of success from other parents or from our families. But it's important to think consciously about your definition of success if you have a child who learns differently.

Dr. Edward Hallowell, founder of the Hallowell Centers and a NY Times bestselling author of books about Attention Deficit Disorder (ADD), has both dyslexia and ADHD. One of his most powerful messages is that school performance doesn't predict performance as an adult.[42]

Dr. Hallowell also warns that treating children with LDs as though they are sick or broken often makes children feel like failures, even when we're trying to help.

Avoid making decisions for your child's life because of pity. Make decisions because you're looking forward, and setting up an environment that can shape your child into a good, happy adult.

What Qualities Bring Success?

Many experts encourage us to identify talents and strengths at the same time as we're identifying learning problems. And then parents are encouraged to build those strengths. But parents report being confused and frustrated by the "strength" question: how do we support, or even identify strengths when our child isn't an expert violinist, or able to do gymnastics at an early age?

Experts aren't talking about the ability to bring home more gold medals when they talk about childhood strengths. Instead, they are talking about old-fashioned character development. In his essay, *Their Beautiful Minds*, Hallowell suggests that the most important qualities to look for in a child are: "confidence, enthusiasm, the ability to persist in the face of disappointment, the ability to ask for and give help, spunk, a sense of humor, courage, ambition, the ability to take responsibility and the ability to do the right thing when no one is looking."

These qualities, he says, are the real predictors of who will do well in life.

The Frostig Center of Pasadena published results from a 20-year study of what makes people with LD successful. They identified six attributes found in successful people, and produced a guide called "Life Success for Students with Learning Disabilities: A Parent's Guide."[43] The qualities they discovered lead to success are:

- Self-awareness.
- Proactivity
- Perseverance
- Goal setting
- Use of social support systems
- Emotional coping strategies

Not one of these attributes requires a school for development. As a matter of fact, your child can work to develop these attributes while doing things like sports, family outings, hobbies, and volunteering in the community. But what *doesn't* develop those attributes is relentless failure. And too often, relentless failure is what LD children encounter at school.

In his speech at the "Beat the Odds" Summit at the White House, Google's Global Education Evangelist, Jaime Casap, suggested that, instead of asking your child what she wants to do when she grows up, talk with her about what's going on in the world and ask her what problem she wants to solve. Then ask her how she will accomplish her goals.[44]

In addition to talking about the world, reach out and expose your child to other people who have a passion for what they do. Hopes, dreams, and passion will help to lift your child to his own success. Many parents report that it was their children who taught them the definition of real success. Make sure to leave the door open to new directions.

In 2015, the National Center for Learning Disabilities released a report called "Student Voices: A Study of Young Adults with Learning and Attention Issues." The report summarized research from two decades of following young LD children as they transitioned into adulthood—and studying what caused children to be more or less successful.[45]

The study concluded that speaking up counts, mentoring helps, community connections make young people stronger, and that "having a confident and capable parent is strongly associated with young adult transition success." It's important for parents to stay strong and positive. We're in this for the long run, and our health, positive outlook, and support mean the world for our children.

Where Does Failure Fit in?

Failure is tricky when you're the parent of a child with LD. In fact, Chapter 2, "Protect Your Child," starts by stating that relentless failure is bad for children. But there's a big difference between relentless failure in no-win situations, and ordinary stumbles that happen all the time. Relentless failure, with no possibility of success, sucks motivation and spirit away from a child. Mistakes and teachable moments, however, are some of the most valuable lessons of childhood.

Parents of children with LDs are often in "protection mode." Sometimes our children have uneven competencies, so we have to keep watch, quietly help, and make sure that our child has an opportunity to succeed in his environment. But even while we do that, we need to actively search for situations that will build character.

Remember when your child was learning to walk? She kept falling and trying, until she succeeded. She didn't quit. And she did it herself. Every child has that drive when they're young. It's important for children to keep that drive, for them to see failure as a step in the process, not the destination. It's also important that children don't learn to sit passively, waiting for a parent to step in. When your daughter finally learned to walk after all of those bumps, she felt awesome!

Our attitude toward failure is one of the things that gives us a sense of well-being: the ability to move on and succeed. The ability to fail—and to learn from failure and keep going—is one of the secrets to success. Tips on failure from other parents:

- Expect a lot from your child. We should expect our children to cook, clean, and do laundry, and other chores.[46] Even if your child has a hard week with spelling, she can do a wonderful job washing the laundry or helping the family by putting away the dishes. Don't take those successes away.[47]

- Put your hands in your pockets and let your child do things by herself. If she makes mistakes, keep your hands in your pockets while you ask her to identify what failed, and how she will fix it. Say "What's the problem? How will you fix it?" Then let her do it. Yes, it will take much longer. That's OK.

- If your child hates to lose, use rock-paper-scissors or dice competitions to decide everything. When you set up lots of little tiny you-might-fail situations, with immediate try-agains, it can help to remove "I might fail" as the focus.

Children are smart. The best way to build a child's self-esteem is for that child to try to succeed at something that is genuinely challenging. Keep an eye out for these opportunities.

All children experience failure, but for children who learn differently, failure is built into the system. It's your job to create opportunities for and pathways to success, not to simply prevent failure. Resilience in the face of failure can be exercised in many different parts of a child's life. Take opportunities to let your child experience and own some failures and to think through and create solutions right from the beginning. It will pay off.

Working with Professionals

It takes more than one person to help a child with LDs. When you talk with teachers and school administrators, educate yourself so that you feel confident enough to bring your own opinions to the table. Chances are they have never had a child exactly like yours, so you're bringing them new knowledge.

You may decide to hire a specialist or a tutor to help your child learn. If you do this, it makes a lot of sense to look for professionals who work well with your child and communicate well with you. Ask tutors if they have worked with LD children. Many tutors just do homework with children. If your child has real problems with the basics, however, doing homework might not be the best way to help them learn. Some tutors will map out a learning strategy for your child. Chapter 7, "What They Don't Teach You About Learning Differences," gives an overview of working with therapists.

It's important to educate yourself on your child's LD. Read the books and identify the experts. Remember that you can set up a phone call to interview specialists, including doctors. And it's important to get second opinions. Three things to remember:

- Sometimes people who are great with kids aren't so great with adults.

- You can always change your mind.

- Sometimes you can hire a professional just for an hour to help you understand something.

Be a Smart Consumer

When you go in to talk with a doctor, it's a good idea to research beforehand, and write down your questions. If you have questions about different diagnoses or therapies, search for reputable studies or articles about them online and print them out. You can refer to them when you talk to your doctor. Evaluate information critically.

Be a smart consumer of medical information.[48] The National Institute of Health's MedlinePlus website advises consumers to consider the source. If you're on a website, look at the "About Us" page. Who runs the site? Is information reviewed before it is posted? Be skeptical. Things that sound too good to be true often are. The best thing to look for is current, unbiased information based on scientific research. Look to see if the type of therapy or treatment is involved in any studies.

A reputable study is one that is in a peer-reviewed medical journal. A reputable article usually appears in a large newspaper or magazine with a national distribution (not just a special interest blog), and it usually references or is based upon studies, or a doctor's own work.

Parents say that it's a good idea to ask if professionals "believe in" things like dyslexia and sensory processing, and select the professionals who say that they do. Both of those diagnoses have been around for 30 years, and a doctor who doesn't believe in them is a doctor who doesn't read new studies and update his or her world view.

Set up Goals

If you do start working with outside professionals or therapists, as described in Chapter 7, talk with them first about how they work. Be careful about therapists who charge many thousands of dollars up front, with no goals, and no guarantees. While most therapies don't offer guarantees, there are many therapists who will let you quit if it's not working out.

With therapists such as occupational therapists and vision therapists, the child's skills are measured at the beginning of a therapy session, and then goals are set and a therapy plan is set up. In both types of therapy, many therapists give homework, because it's better to stimulate the brain every day, than it is once a week. You can ask if your therapist does this.

Many parents will schedule a "therapy round" of three months. They set goals with the therapist at the start, and then check them afterwards to see if the therapy has been effective. Then they start a new activity or therapy for the next three months.

You Make the Decisions

Parents know and understand many things about what their children go through physically, socially, and educationally. Your knowledge and input has value. As parents, you're ultimately responsible for raising your child, and only you have the "whole picture." You're the decision maker for your child.

- If you need to bring in people to give you advice, do it.
- If you don't understand something, ask to have it explained to you.

- If you want to know what a professional recommends, ask them—and then ask them questions about their answer. If you don't understand, tell them you need more time.

Managing Information and Efforts

If your child has problems in school, you should immediately begin saving information about your child's school experience in an organized fashion. In order to help your child, it's quite possible that you will deal with the educational, medical, insurance, and legal systems. All of these systems require organized information.

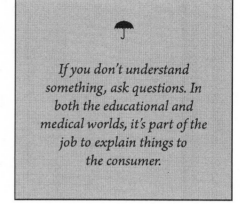

If you don't understand something, ask questions. In both the educational and medical worlds, it's part of the job to explain things to the consumer.

- School, doctors, and insurance system require structured records.
- Organizing information and prioritizing concerns help you take advantage of your time with teachers and other experts.
- Establishing goals with professionals helps keep them accountable.
- Gathering information in one place helps you track growth and gains that happen over longer periods of time.

For more information on how saved information is valuable, see Chapter 5, "Claiming Support in the School System."

What Tools Work Best for Saving Information?

Although our world is now full of apps and software, most parents report that, when they manage their child's information, two favorite tools are still paper-based: a support binder and a paper calendar.

Your Child's Support Binder

You might live in email, but if you work to get support for your child in the educational system, sooner or later you'll end up in a meeting where you'll have to pull out a piece of paper and pass it around. Not only do the educational system, and a large part of the medical system still use paper, but your exhibits might well be first or second-grade writing and spelling tests. Because of this, you really can't beat a large, 1.5" three-ring binder in for storing information.

You can buy this at any office supply store, where you should also purchase binder tabs and pockets.

Calendar

Many parents use a small paper calendar to track dates that pertain to their child's education. Some parents use their calendar to track teacher meetings and conversations. If the teacher tells you that she's trying a new technique, you can mark on the calendar when she changes her approach, and then keep samples of your child's work to see if the technique is effective. If you choose to hire a tutor or a specialist, you can track the experience on this calendar as well. A paper calendar is good, because you can pull it out during meetings.

What Information Should You Track?

Parents often divide "managing school" into two parts. The first part is talking with the teacher and supporting your child, and the second part is formally claiming support, as described in Chapter 5. You'll need to keep good records for both. Here are some types of information to track:

- Learn and track your child's challenges in the school world. Are his challenges just for reading, math, sitting still? How are his social skills? Can he remember things? What's hard for him to learn? It's very common to discover that your child has more challenges than just one. Appendix C, "The Whole-Child Diagnostic Approach," describes all of the ways in which a child can be evaluated for LDs. Keep those categories in mind and try to gather information about every area that is a challenge. Collect examples, write dates and explanations on the back, and put them in a binder. Use tabs to arrange information by date.

- You can keep all test results and use them to monitor progress. It's important to realize that most tests don't measure in a parallel fashion, and it can be difficult to compare results of two different tests.

- Teachers commonly use a plan for what they are teaching, called a *curriculum*. If you can talk your teacher into sharing her curriculum with you, you can not only try to prepare your child in advance for what will be presented, but you can also track what part of the curriculum is difficult for your child. This provides valuable feedback to your teacher and might help detect patterns of learning trouble.

- If homework is an issue, keep track of how long your child spends on homework, and whether or not you need to re-teach your child at night. Also keep track of what homework is sent home. If homework is too difficult to do, or is presented in a way that is particularly difficult for your child, make a copy of it and write why, either on a sticky note, or on the back of the paper. If you change the homework to make it easier, track what you do and if it works. Some parents take pictures of homework, to track what's difficult to learn.

- Finally, keep all communications from the teacher or school, including report cards, tests, any notes home, and any emails. If you have a conversation with a teacher, specialist, or administrator, email them later that day, summarizing the conversation ("Just so I got it right"), then print out the email and put it into your binder. Not only does summarizing help you and the professional communicate better, you are laying the framework for the legal process of claiming support for your child, as described in Chapter 5.

- You can request accommodations so that homework and schoolwork are presented in a way that your child can better understand. You can also share information with future teachers or tutors so they can see what works and what doesn't. See "Be a

Detective: Researching a Learning Profile," and "Working with Accommodations and Modifications," in Chapter 4.

You Matter

It's important to realize that part of this journey is yours, and that it's separate from your child's journey. Here are some things that will help you in your journey.

Take Care of Yourself

In an airplane, they teach you to put your oxygen mask on before trying to help your children. But if your child is having issues, the last thing that gets mentioned is support for the parent. Parents of children with LDs often report stress and parental distress.[49]

It's very important that you take time off to recharge your battery. Keep in touch with friends, find an interest other than parenting, and take a break. Some parents benefit from reaching out to a therapist, or taking an exercise class, or booking the occasional weekend off. Working yourself to the bone will only give you less resilience to support your child and family.

Remember back when your child was an infant and you got no sleep? You did that, and you can do this.

Don't Panic

In today's parenting world, we're encouraged to panic over everything. Pause and breathe. School and child-raising are both full of false pressures. Take a hard look at pressures, for both you and your child. Most of them don't matter as much as you might think.

Everything that is taught in grammar school is re-taught multiple times. This means that your child can step off of the pressurized homework merry-go-round for a while so that she can take time to learn the skills and building blocks for success. Ask questions and push back.

Every parent makes mistakes. You'll make all sorts of them, because your child's situation is unique and every LD parent is forced to use a trial-and-error approach. Don't obsess over mistakes. Let go, take it as a growth experience, and move forward. You're modeling behavior for your child. If one thing doesn't work, try something new.

Don't let school system problems make you crazy. Remember: If your child needs more time, push for it. Your child has more time to mature and learn than it might seem. It's not too late.

Develop and Nurture Your Own Big Picture

One way to help your child develop success attributes, and possibly balance out a difficult school experience, is to remember that you have life goals larger than school, and to bring those goals into your life. What are your family's values, and what do they mean in the world? What's really important to you and your family? Travel? Building things? Fishing? Show your children the enjoyment that you get from being with family, doing a job well, helping others, and doing what you love.

What did your parents and grandparents do? What made them happy and successful? Try to connect personal characteristics with a person's path in life. Keep an eye out for pathways and supportive communities for your child.

Talk with your children about life, happiness, and success. Talk about current events or inventions at the dinner table every night. Do good in the world. Tell jokes. Use every opportunity to model the behavior that you would like to see in your child. Talk about your own frustrations or mistakes and how you will deal with them. Show your child how you blow off steam.

Finally, remove your family and child from the academic situation periodically and take a vacation. Especially for LD children, there is so much more to life than academic stress! And no, don't make your child do daily homework during every vacation. Your child works extremely hard. Give him (and yourself) regular life-breaks. Clear your heads.

Many people who have taken their children on vacation report that simply going to a new place is very stimulating for their children. Brains grow in all directions, all the time. Mix it up. Stressed brains learn less. And remember, strengths that will carry your child to a successful, happy life are often formed by developing interests far away from academics, like sports, the outdoors, and family fun.

Make Balance a Priority

There is a lot of balancing that needs to go on in our lives. Here are the most important areas to look out for.

- **Work and fun**— Studies show that children learn more when they're having fun.[50] Children's brains develop constantly, stimulated by such things as being read to, cooking with mom or dad, and rolling down a hill. Play is what develops a child's brain. It's good to do schoolwork, but kids need free time too.

- **Computers and physical time**— Studies almost universally say that it's best to severely limit computer game time.[51] Some parents do this with a "no computers during the week" rule. Other parents limit time and make children play outside first. Best limit? No more than two hours on the computer, ever.

- **Attention between siblings**— Give each child some special alone time with you every week. Make sure every action and decision doesn't seem to revolve around your child's LD. Highlight strengths and interests of all siblings. A family dinner, where you share challenges, accomplishments, and what you've learned, or the day's highs and lows, is a great way to let all siblings participate and learn from one another.

- **Time with family and spouse**— Raising a child with an LD can be stressful. A date night can set things up for fun with your spouse without stress. You can also bring in a "mother's helper" during the day on a weekend, who can play with your child, giving you relaxation time at home. Invest in your relationship by gifting one another with undivided attention. And don't forget to laugh.

- **Giving and getting**— Your child will be getting a lot of help. One way to feel good about yourself is to offer help to others in return.

Keep an eye out for volunteer activities that will help your child and family feel valuable to the community and offer her a chance to give back.

- **A schedule too heavy in therapy can send a negative message to your child—** Don't just feed your child a steady diet of "fix me" classes. A good rule of thumb is to have a maximum of one or two therapy classes a week, and to balance them with plenty of fun and down time, supporting friendship-building and interests. Children need to play.

More than anything else, take a breath, calm down, and realize that this is not a race. Take the time that you need.

The Power of Community: Joining Support Groups

It can be challenging and isolating to support a child with LDs.[52] Sometimes the best thing you can do is talk with parents who share your experience. The right parenting groups can change your life.

An online parenting group might have members online 24 hours a day with ideas, understanding, and resources. A local group might help you find other parents with similar children, who can gather for playdates, or perhaps just a mom's night out. Studies confirm that support groups can help with the stress of LD parenting.[53]

During the LD journey, it's natural to spend a lot of time and energy worrying and looking for answers. And even your closest friend or family member isn't always able to help with some of the problems and questions you may have while parenting an LD child.

A parenting community or support group selects itself. Everyone in the group is deeply interested in this topic, and many have walked in your shoes. Learning to reach out to a support group can result in friendships and shared, deep interests.

Support groups can look like anything. Beth Berry, author of the "Revolution from Home" blog, recently wrote about how mothers who "lack a village" struggle. Her suggestions include becoming an integral part of something. "Whether it's a knitting group, dance troupe, church, kayaking club, or homeschool collective, commit to growing community around one area of your life that enlivens you or fills a need," she says. [54]

What Do Support Groups Offer?

Ideas for Effective Parenting
Every child is a unique bundle of maturity, likes and dislikes, skills, passions, and challenges—and that's just the start. Parents you meet in a support group will often be able to tell you what worked for their child and how it tied in with their specific needs.

Learn about Successes
In a support group, you can meet parents who have raised children like yours, or adults who have the same learning profile as your child. Meeting and hearing about their successes can help both you and your child.

Get Referrals and Suggestions
Since you can explain your exact situation in a support group, users will often tell you exactly what (or who) they used for their similar situation. It's a great way to get a referral or suggestion, for everything from a doctor, to a book, a therapy, or even a technique.

Reduce Stress
Sharing your feelings is a proven method of managing stress.[55] Helping other people can also reduce stress, so the natural sharing as you talk in a parent support group can help you take care of yourself.

Finding or Starting Your Own Support Group

You can find an online support group by searching for one on Facebook or the internet. Often groups will have different personalities, and it might take a few tries before you find one you like. Look for a group that is private.[56] You don't want your information made public.

You can look for a group in your area starting at your child's school, non-profit organizations for LDs, or local learning centers. You can also ask a local therapist or specialist to connect you with similar parents, or work with a local parent's club. An example of a local group is the Berkeley Parents Network.[57] An example of a regional group is the Peninsula Parents of Special Needs Kids group.[58]

If there is no group in your area, parents suggest that you start our own. It can be as easy as sending an email or you can create a Facebook page, make it private, and invite other parents.

And you don't have to just ask people in your child's school, either. You can ask around at the grocery store, at your dentist, or anywhere you talk with other people. You'll be shocked at how many people "know someone" whose child has an LD. You are not alone.

You can also post a notice on local bulletin boards, giving your phone number or email address as a contact.

If you do set up a group, you can set up park days, lunches or coffee with other parents, and you can use the group to share useful information. It's important to find other local parents who can give you teacher feedback, and recommendations for therapists or tutors. Personal experience is valuable.

Upgrading Your Parenting Skills

We all know parents who are gifted organizers, set limits with ease, have high-achieving, polite children, and seem perfect. Guess what? Even those parents often ask for help when their children have LDs. Each challenge presented by a child with an LD is an opportunity for teaching and learning, but it can be hard to come up with a consistent, positive approach when you're overwhelmed.

We all know that children change. One maturity level responds well to a specific type of parenting, but the next maturity level might prove utterly confusing until you figure out what works. You'd buy a special tool to fix a car or the roof, wouldn't you? Parenting classes are a special tool that can save you time and pain.

For each stage of your child's life, if you've thought through goals and situations beforehand, and can stay calm and consistent during parenting situations, your parenting is more effective. If you feel blindsided or emotionally overwhelmed, if you find yourself blowing up, or if your children don't listen, it might be time to consider a parenting class, seminar, or online coach. A parenting class can give you a new toolkit for taking care of your child.

Resource organizations in your area often have a list of classes. The *Fine Until Kindergarten* website has a bonus list of parenting classes that you can find at www.fineuntilkindergarten.com/bonus.

CHAPTER 4:
Helping Your Child Succeed in School

Most children currently identified as "learning disabled" are literally wired to learn differently than most other children Given the brain's incredible resourcefulness, in most cases these differences need never become disabling—unless we let them.

—*Dr. Fernette and Dr. Brock Eide, The Mislabeled Child*

The way that we discover learning differences is fairly brutal. You spend 5 years at home and in preschool with your creative and happy child. School starts and all of a sudden, your child learns that she can't do things. Your child, who is still learning how to socialize and act in a classroom, begins to realize that something is wrong—with her.

It's common for children to start the school year excited and happy. But LD parents talk about watching their children develop embarrassment and humiliation, as they realize that other children "get" things and they don't. This shift—from happiness to sadness—is one of the indicators of an LD.

Unfortunately, there is no smooth process by which our society identifies an LD child and says "Your child's brain works differently. We know that he can learn just fine, if we teach him differently. We'll do this."

As a part of their job, teachers from preschool through grammar school are required to identify children[59] who demonstrate learning disabilities.[60] Children who display LD are supposed to be observed, tested, and (by law) provided equal access to a "free and appropriate education."[61] It sounds good, but in reality, it's a pretty bumpy process.

Our system doesn't automatically test children who have trouble in school. When children do get tested, they're often just tested for one thing, not broadly tested for potential LDs. Some school districts refuse to acknowledge that particular LDs exist. School districts don't provide support for all types of LD. And, since each child with an LD is unique, teachers and parents often must use trial and error to be effective.

In this unclear environment, the parent must turn into a kind of project manager, making sure that their child's needs are met, and that the process to support their child continues, throughout different teachers, different grades, and even different schools.

Partnering with Your Child's Teacher

Your child's teacher is one of the most important people in his life. Every year, especially during the first years of school, your child will spend hours in an environment that is controlled by the teacher. It's important to make sure that the teacher has all of the information she needs in order to be effective working with your child.

Get to know your child's teacher at the beginning of every year. After all, the two of you will team up to make your child successful. Your job is to to provide information for the teacher, negotiate expectations at a top level, if necessary, track your child's performance, and provide support.

Today's teachers often have up to 30 students in their classrooms, so if you want the teacher to have specific, important information about your child, many parents choose to send an introductory letter during the first week of school, as described below.

Making Teacher Relationships Effective

Here are some tips from experienced parents for making teacher relationships work smoothly.

- Be friendly. Don't overshare. Stick to just a few talking points.

- Teachers have a natural guard up against emotional parents. The minute you become emotional, you lose ground. Keep emotion out of the situation, no matter what happens.

- Treat this like a job. If the teacher dresses up, do the same (a little less than she does.) If she doesn't dress up, then be more casual, but not sloppy. Be respectful of her needs.

- Don't barge into her classroom. Make appointments. At the same time, keep your eyes open. Some parents admit to showing up a bit early and looking around to see how their child is doing.

  If you are nervous about a class, you can always request to observe by sitting in the classroom. (You will never get a clear view if you do this, since both teacher and your child will behave differently if you are around. Sometimes parents hire a professional to observe.)

- Use very few words. What's the most important thing to tell her? Letters should be as short as you can get them and should only talk about one or two points. She's busy and has many other students. Conversations should touch on one or two points.

- Prioritize. You can't get everything. Remember what your top priorities are in this class and mention those concerns first.

- Some experienced parents always show up with a coffee. If you do this, make it low-key.

- If the teacher uses a new technique or tries something and it works, keep track of it in your notes, and be sure to let her know. Positive feedback is always appreciated.

- And of course always thank her for the time and the effort she is spending with you and your child.

Teacher Assignments

In general, keep an eye out for teachers who are kind and will try to help your child. If you discover a wonderful teacher in the next grade up, sometimes it's a good idea to go right to the principal and ask for that teacher for the coming year.

- It's a lot less trouble to diplomatically ask for what you want in the first place, than it is to ask for your child to be moved or supported because the year is a failure.

- You'll never be able to find the perfect teacher. Everyone is human. You want to avoid teachers who might actively harm your child. Secondly, you want to find a teacher who will support your child's learning needs, especially if they have had training in how to teach children with LD.

- If you fear your child has been assigned a teacher who is a poor fit, remember that one child's unfriendly teacher can be another child's favorite teacher. Some unlikely teacher/student pairings end up being magically positive.

- Fears aren't enough of a reason to move your child. If you want to move your child out of a classroom, document problems, concerns, and conversations. Remember that you have a limited number of requests that you can make. What if you ask for your child to be moved and the new teacher is no better? If possible, try to work things out first.

- If the situation is not working out, and the teacher isn't following the 504 or IEP, or isn't responsive, feel free to meet with the principal. Stay pleasant, but tenacious. Sometimes a principal can help to straighten things out with a teacher. If things are bad enough to move classes, state your worries and then ask specifically for an alternative placement and tell the principal which teacher you want and why. Finally, if the school isn't following an IEP, you can file a complaint, as described in "Disagreeing with the School and System" in Chapter 5.

Meeting with Teachers Before School Starts

Sometimes parents want or need to speak with teachers or school administrators in the weeks right before school starts. Although you shouldn't do it unless you need to, you might want a meeting like this because your child had issues last year, or your child is transitioning to another school and you want to meet the team. Another reason for a meeting is teacher assignment.

You can email a teacher to see if she's available to meet before school starts for the year. If you do this, it's a good idea to email your introduction letter first, and then ask for a meeting. You can also talk with the counselor, to see if the teacher is available, and the counselor can help to set up a meeting. If the teacher is resistant, don't push it.

Writing an Introductory Letter

An introductory letter will help the teacher meet your child's needs, even if your child doesn't have a *504 or IEP*. Your letter should be professional and positive. You don't want to prejudice the teacher against your child by sounding like he's going to be hard to teach. At the same time,

The 504 plan and IEP are legal documents that specify how your child's education is supported in school.

you want the teacher to know that you're here to support your child and her.

Parents recommend the following tips for your letter:

Chapter 6, "School Support Programs for LD," describes the IEP and 504 plan, and Chapter 5, "Claiming Support in the School System," explains how to request testing and claim support.

- Keep it short. Pretend that the letter is a summary for an executive. Don't explain everything, just mention the most important three or so points and leave the door open for future conversations.

- Make the letter pleasant, to emphasize that you're on the same team and you're looking forward to working with the teacher.

- Many parents say that they're checking to make sure the teacher received the 504 plan or IEP (if applicable).

- Mention one or two things your child loves or is good at: "I want to introduce my son, John. John is in chorus, loves to draw, and plays baseball very well. He is empathetic and loves to help."

- What are your child's learning issues? Anything you can say about them? (e.g. "James has *dysgraphia*, which means that he can think much faster and better than he can write. This is very frustrating for him, because he knows answers, but it's very difficult for him to write them down.")

- If your son had problems last year with remembering homework, you can mention it by saying "I would like to meet with you to set up support for remembering homework. I would like to know how you typically handle this."

- If you do have specific suggestions or requests, it's often more effective when the suggestions come from a doctor or other professional, rather than from you. (For example, "Last year, James' teacher, Mrs. Wilson, performed a binder check after school every day. That worked well, and she suggested that we do it this year.") You can also put suggestions into a *learning profile*, as described below.

Appendix E contains a sample introductory letter.

Creating and Using a Learning Profile

A *learning profile* is a short, one-page summary that tells the teacher how your child learns and succeeds, and what teaching methods and approaches work best for your child. Unlike other education-based reference documents, your child's learning profile doesn't just summarize test results and weaknesses.

A learning profile is different than an introductory letter. You can use both, although some parents choose to use one or the other. The learning profile is not a personal letter. It looks like a professional tool for the teacher to use and is meant to be used year after year, as an updatable reference page. You can think of it as "teaching shortcuts for my child's success," and you can laminate it, to emphasize it as a tool.

In a world where we're encouraged to use strength-based parenting and teaching approaches, a learning profile helps identify positive paths to success. You spend a significant portion of your life tracking what doesn't work for your child, so a learning profile can be fun to create. What works?

A Learning Profile Helps Prioritize and Shape Teaching Methods

It's very common for young LD children to have problems acquiring skills, displaying behaviors, and producing output. Sometimes, a child has processing problems and needs more time. Many teaching methods focus on identifying weaknesses, and then strengthening them. If a child has an LD, however, focusing on weaknesses can lead to repeated failure and frustration for both teacher and child.

LD children often need outside therapy, specific training, or a higher level of maturity to learn a basic skill, as described in Chapter 7, "What

They Don't Tell You About Learning Differences." Some children will never learn specific skills, and will have to just work around them as adults. If your child's brain isn't ready to learn spelling, handwriting, or to memorize math facts, more effort won't always make a difference.

As the parent of a child with LD, you will learn to look at educational circumstances and ask questions like "What's the point of this assignment?" If the point is to demonstrate ideas, then your child should be able to type, or make a video, or a collage, or a drawing. You'll learn to push back.

This shift—away from focusing so much on the remedial (handwriting, spelling, and grammar) that the lesson gets lost, to changing a lesson so that a child can learn what he is able to learn at this time, can be difficult. It's not how schools usually teach, and some teachers have never tried to teach in this way. A learning profile can help make this shift happen.

One very experienced mom of a boy who had diagnosed, severe dysgraphia, Shannon, finally wrote a note to her son's teacher, saying "Please do not try to FIX him. Your time, and his are much better served if you let ME be the one to worry about his long-term ability to write, and you worry about how to help him get his ideas and answers out of his head without writing or typing. It is a problem that has been addressed in multiple ways for many years and you can rest assured that we, his parents will continue to work on it. You just worry about fifth grade."[62]

This letter is blunt, but it contains a message for how to effectively teach Shannon's son. This information would be great in a learning profile.

Writing a Learning Profile

A learning profile typically contains information about:

- Who is my child? What are her interests, and what motivates her?
- What is my child's primary interest?

- What is my child's biggest learning strength? Has she surprised you with her knowledge in any particular field?
- Has she been diagnosed with any LD? Do you suspect any others?
- What are her biggest challenges in the classroom? (Including things like anxiety.) And what helps with them?
- How does my child learn best? What's the best way for my child to receive and learn information? (visual, auditory, kinesthetic)
- What's the best way for my child to display learning? (writing, speaking, artwork), for measuring learning.
- In what classroom circumstances does my child work *best*? (with a partner, alone, front of room)

In addition, the profile should talk about tips for getting a child to succeed (e.g. if she feels awkward, give her a job or ask her to make a drawing), and list some things that the child loves, so that the teacher will have an easy time connecting with her.

Here are some ways to describe alternate techniques for demonstrating learning.

To measure this ability:	These alternate techniques worked to show learning:
Reading comprehension	Can explain verbally, use a scribe, do a drawing or a fill in a mind map. Can show in a flowchart or make a video.
Memorizing lists	Can explain why the lists are necessary, color a simple diagram showing why the list matters, and can refer to a color-coded list.
Writing essays	Can draw or diagram the essay. Can learn and show main sentence and supporting arguments in a picture. Can tell the essay verbally. Can describe elements of the essay separately: main characters, plotline. Can create a comic.
Spelling	Best to work on identifying phonics in a word (e.g. underline the middle sound). Best to work on words that all show the same spelling pattern.

To measure this ability:	These alternate techniques worked to show learning:
Memorizing sequenced information (e.g. math)	Can draw her own multiplication table and use it to solve problems. Can learn a song with gestures for simple memorization. Can work on number sense.[63] Can use story-based flashcards.

You can encourage your child to develop her own separate learning profile.[64] She can draw a picture and list her goals and worries for the year. She can also mention what worked best last year and what she is most excited about learning. And she can include a drawing of a loved pet or accomplishment.

At the end of every year, you can ask this year's teacher to write up the three most effective things they did to teach your child. This is a way of passing child-specific wisdom on to the next teacher, and a great idea if you have a unique learner. You can also use this as teacher recommendations for the coming year.

Be a Detective: Researching a Learning Profile

If you have a professional test your child, or you apply for an IEP through the school district, you'll be able to gather information through the testing process (see Chapter 5). You will naturally gather information about what works every night as you try various methods on homework. And you already know many things about how your child learns, what he needs for success, and what techniques help him succeed. One source of information about test results is a book by the founders of the Wrightslaw.com website, called *All About Tests and Assessments*.[65]

The type of professional who can help you create a learning profile is called an *educational consultant*. An educational consultant helps you to look through the results of your child's psycho-educational evaluations and translate them into action. Dan Leibowitz, M.Ed., MS. Sped., CET, is the owner of Innovative Learning Services in Kentfield,

California. He suggests you start by requesting a thorough and clear debrief, either with the professional who did the testing or someone who is skilled at interpreting and communicating about it. The next step, says Dan, is to get help transforming the test results into a manageable, concrete plan of action with measurable goals that everyone, including the student, agrees upon - for both the school and home environments. You don't have to wait for an IEP meeting to begin establishing a plan.

Dan emphasizes that often, students are not necessarily coached well in understanding their learning needs and how to become more successful. A learning profile can remind parents, children, and teachers about what works best.

Learning from Homeschooling Parents

Cindy Gaddis is author of a book called *The Right Side of Normal*. For years, she has hosted a large internet user group[66] and given seminars to parents who look for different ways to support their children's learning. Cindy is a research-driven mother of seven children whom she describes as being "creative, bright, intense, high-maintenance, and interesting." Cindy homeschooled her children, some of whom had LD issues, and documented how she modified her teaching methods to be effective. In particular, one paragraph stands out:

"I have a right-brained *artist* son who is strong with both auditory and visual inputs, and is less strong in the spatial area. My right-brained *builder* son, on the other hand, [has good spatial skills], and seeks a kinesthetic input, but is weak with auditory and ...visual input."

Gaddis has spent time really watching her children as they learn, and she's been able to put together a learning profile that lets her be most effective in teaching each child. Notice that she's characterized each child with his particular interest or gift. One child is an artist, and the other is a builder. Does your child have a defining interest?

If your child is tested for LDs, you'll be able to go through test results to determine cognitive strengths and weaknesses. It's good to choose, as Gaddis did, two stronger, and two weaker skills for a profile.

Many parents with LD children are homeschooling, and are posting what they learn on the internet. You can search for the term "Homeschooling" and your child's diagnosis to look for teaching approaches that might work with your child.

A diagnosis is not a plan for success. It's important to watch how your child learns and experiences life, and to communicate information that can help a teacher to teach him.

Working with Accommodations and Modifications

An *accommodation* allows a student to complete an assignment without changing the quantity of skill level of the work. An example accommodation is use of a computer for writing, graphic organizer, or more time. LD children need accommodations for two main reasons.

A *modification* allows a student to complete an assignment, but simplifies or changes the quantity or skill level of the work required. An example modification is fewer math or spelling questions, different questions, shorter writing assignments, and teacher-provided notes or study guides.

Your child is eligible for accommodations and modifications both with a 504 plan and with an IEP. Occasionally, teachers will provide accommodations and support for undiagnosed children. However, there's no guarantee that next year's teacher will provide support, so it's a good idea to have your child diagnosed and claim support.

There are people who claim that "accommodations aren't fair." And LD parents often reply with "LDs aren't fair either." But the fact is that our legal system has acknowledged LDs as disabilities while our child is in school, and our children are absolutely entitled to the legal support extended to them.

Why Do We Use Accommodations?

The way we teach means that our children must first master fundamental skills, then use those skills to learn. If a child cannot master a fundamental skill, however, she is often prevented from learning. Fundamental skills include: paying attention, listening, understanding words, reading from a book or a board, writing to convey thoughts, taking notes from a whiteboard, or comprehending symbols, whether alphabet or numerical.

The simplest tasks are often the hardest for LD children, and early grades don't give children access to tools that we all take for granted: calculators, keyboards, even a cellphone that lets students snap pictures of a whiteboard so they can remember.

If you look around you today, we all routinely use use tools for support: for reading, writing, dictation, reminders, and task lists. Knowing how to master the proper tool is important for success.

Some of the most common tools and techniques that can allow children to learn around their learning differences are:

- Using a printed multiplication table,
- Taking tests in a separate room,
- Dictating answers and paragraphs to a scribe,
- Using audio books.

Choosing Accommodations

While teachers and the IEP or 504 team may have some ideas about accommodations, it is the job of the parent to research similar situations, and find out what type of accommodations will support their child best. This can be an overwhelming job, but remember: the fewer the better! Long lists can overwhelm teachers.

Parents suggest that you really pay attention to the problems that your child is having, and then look for accommodations to help with those problems. Then you should spend a little bit of time researching what accommodations parents of children like yours recommend. Pinterest is one location that has a lot of recommendations for accommodations and teaching support.[67]

There are many lists of accommodations on the internet for all different types of LD, such as:

- Auditory Processing[68]
- Dyslexia[69]
- Sensory Integration[70]
- Dysgraphia[71]

Children with learning differences often need creative and diverse methods and tools. Most teachers aren't trained in exactly which method would be good for your child, so you'll need to make sure that information about your child's needs is documented for the school—and supplied to the teacher.

Describing Accommodations

There are different ways to describe accommodations. One list of accommodations [72] from the University of Buffalo's Assistive Technology Training Online Project, is very wordy. Here's an example goal:

Provide this Student with Low-Distraction Work Areas

- Provide this student with a quiet, distraction free area for quiet study time and test-taking. It is the responsibility of the teacher to take the initiative to privately and discreetly (do not draw peer attention to the student) "send" this student to a quiet, distraction-free room/area for each testing session. It is important to assure that once the student begins a task requiring a quiet, distraction-free environment that no interruptions be permitted until the student is finished.

- Always seat this student near the source of instruction and/or stand near student when giving instructions in order to help the student by reducing barriers and distractions between him and the lesson. For this reason it is important to encourage the student to sit near positive role models to ease the distractions from other students with challenging or diverting behaviors.

This list of general accommodations, on the other hand, is a simple list, created by an experienced mother. [73] It's comprehensive, clear, and short, including things like:

504 Accommodations

- give extra time to complete tasks
- simplify complex directions
- hand worksheets out one at a time
- reduce the reading level of the assignments
- require fewer correct responses to achieve grade (quality vs. quantity)
- allow student to tape record assignments/homework
- provide a structured routine in written form

Teachers are all different, but most would probably rather get a short, clear list than long, detailed instructions. You'll have to decide for your child's situation: what's the most effective way to get the teacher to support your child?

Before You Claim Support: Gather Information

The teacher is usually the first to notice that a child is having trouble, although some children do a great job of holding things together at school. They are well-behaved, quiet, and slip under the radar. At home, though, these children can display trouble coping with school pressure and doing homework. Nightly crying jags or tantrums, and hours spend dawdling or putting off homework can be signs of trouble learning.

If you're at the beginning of your child's journey, it's common to spend time wondering if your child's issues are "bad enough" to warrant an evaluation, or special support from the educational system. Especially if you don't have an LD yourself, LDs can be difficult to understand. If you suspect that your child has an LD, it's a good idea to push to have it tested. 1 in 8 children have an LD, and parents are not qualified to determine if something is "bad enough" for support.

When you start thinking about getting your child tested, continue talking with your child's teacher, and make sure that you are writing down everything: every meeting, every email, and every instance where your child has problems. Information that you gather will be your most powerful tool in getting help for your child. The "Managing Information and Efforts," section of Chapter 3, "Your Journey," talks about what types of information you should track and where to keep it.

During this stage, talk with the teacher about specific problems. Ask her for her opinion: is this an LD? And then ask how she suggests this be handled in a school setting. You can ask if other children have the same challenges, and if there is any behavior that she thinks is unusual. You can also ask if she has seen LD children with this challenge, and if so, what steps were taken. Make sure that you keep comparing your child's performance to the norm. Gather information showing that your child isn't able to learn at the same level as other children.

Your child's teacher might either talk about specific in-class techniques that she's using, suggest the *Response to Integration* in-school process (RTI) described in Chapter 6, "School Support Programs for LD," or she will recommend that your child be tested. Many times, the school will put together a first-response team (often called by different names) to begin watching your child's performance and suggesting actions. If the teacher suggests additional ways to support your child in the classroom, it's a good idea to write down and track those approaches to see how they work, and to set up another meeting in a month to see how things are going.

As described in Chapter 5, you don't need your teacher's permission to claim support, and you don't need to wait until she finishes trying new and different approaches to help your child learn.

CHAPTER 5:
Claiming Support in the School System

How far different thinkers can go depends to a large extent on the abilities and enthusiasm of the advocates and allies in their lives.

—David Flink, founder of the Eye to Eye nationwide LD/ADHD youth mentoring organization[74]

It can be intimidating and overwhelming to claim support for your child in the school system. But the basic process is not complex. This chapter provides a gentle introduction to how you can begin claiming support.

In this book, Chapter 4, "Helping Your Child Succeed in School," describes how to work with schools so your child can succeed, Chapter 6, "School Support Programs for LD," describes the difference between a 504 plan and an IEP, including benefits and disadvantages, and this chapter describes the *process* of how to claim support.

Why Should You Start by Requesting an IEP?

The IEP request process is often explained as a complex system. Many explanations branch off immediately into descriptions of what might happen and why. But we're explaining it differently:

Parents should not have to be LD experts or feel like we need a legal degree before we can apply for support for our children. The (IDEA) law provides diagnostic and support mechanisms. You don't have to be **sure** that your child has an LD before you start. You do have to see a clear pattern of difficulty, a pattern of inability to learn. And then you need to gather together information to demonstrate that difficulty. If your child is identified with LDs that are protected by law, and if those LDs prevent your child from effectively learning, you can claim support. (See "Educational Testing and Claiming Support," below.)

In this chapter, we recommend that if you think that your child has an LD, you write a letter, requesting an IEP. This starts a formal testing process process to see if your child is eligible for an IEP. Just do it. Let the school do their evaluation.

But what if you think that your child just needs a 504? (as explained in Chapter 6.) We suggest that you request an IEP anyway. There is a lot of false information out there. Many school districts, for example, look people in the eye and tell them that dyslexics aren't eligible for an IEP, even though the word "dyslexia" actually appears in the IDEA law. [75] Or schools routinely tell parents that they've never heard of dysgraphia or dyscalculia. Some schools tell parents that ADHD children aren't eligible for support. And other schools tell parents that their child has to receive F's for two years.[76]

Untrue.

A big reason to ask for an IEP first, with full testing, is that it is a broader evaluation of your child, and LDs are hard to diagnose. It's a good idea to have your child tested fully if you see real problems with learning in the classroom.

Too many parents report waiting for three, four, five years to ask for an IEP, and in the meantime, their child was just given less work, instead of being taught properly. Giving less work isn't an appropriate substitute for teaching. And children respond best when they get appropriate support, early.

Claiming Support is a Legal Maneuver

When you claim LD support, you are exercising your child's legal rights. From the time you start, what is written down is very important. The entire process of claiming support means that you are engaging in a legal and bureaucratic negotiation.

If your child qualifies for help, a team the school provides will set up a legal document that formally regulates how the school treats and teaches your child. If your child qualifies for an IEP, by law, you are part of the IEP team and attend all meetings. The legal documents are called either a 504 plan or an IEP, and they're described in Chapter 6.

It's very common for people to disagree with one another during legal negotiations. One of the reasons why parents sometimes have trouble claiming support for our children is that it's not quite clear where we stop being the nice mommy, sending an apple to the teacher, and start showing up with a lawyer and a stack of papers. Our advice is to stay professional during this process. Start to cultivate your own "executive" approach to dealing with teachers.[77]

Here are more tips from parents who have gone through this:

- The school district is not your friend or your enemy. You are in negotiation. Be pleasant, firm, and low-key.
- Do not get your only advice from employees of the school district. Consult more than one source for advice, including even basic interpretations of what the law says. Even if your school says that something is absolutely not covered, don't just blindly accept that as fact. Look it up. Get alternate opinions and do your own research.

- Every school district is unique. Look for other parents in the school and ask them what it was like to get an IEP in your school district. Ask them who to work with, the most effective approaches, and if there's anything you need to know. In particular, ask them what the most difficult part of the process was for them and how they handled it.

- The school can afford to delay the process. If they delay long enough, your child's learning issues are no longer their problem. Can your child afford to wait? Don't let your child go without help because the school is dragging its feet. If you write a letter asking for official testing and an IEP today, it will automatically start the process of getting an IEP.

Start looking for people who know about IEPs and your school district as soon as possible. Keep the names of these people in your binder (as described in Chapter 3, "Your Journey,"), and call them when you need help, even if it's just for a quick coffee. The culture of LD parents is generous and supportive. And especially when it comes to negotiating out interpretations of law with their school district, parents need help.

Who Is Involved?

These are the primary players as you negotiate for your child to receive support in the educational system.

- **Your child's teacher** is the gateway to and provider of day-to-day support and teaching. She is your first point of contact, and she will be working on methods to teach your child in her class. You will work with her to get your child tested initially.

  You will often work through several steps and meetings with your teacher before your child is referred for diagnosis and support. Your child's teacher will attend any meetings that are held during the process of claiming support.

- **Reading specialists, occupational therapists, speech therapists, and additional credentialed professionals** may work with your child. You are always welcome to ask for qualifications.

For more information on what qualifications should be, see Appendix D, "Types of Doctors and Specialists."

- **The school counselor** may or may not be involved in helping your child settle in and succeed in the school. The counselor is often consulted for behavioral problems or if a child shows signs of emotional distress. Unfortunately, some schools no longer have counselors because of budget constraints.

- **The school psychologist** is a professional with a M.A. in school psychology. Often he or she serves more than one school so is only available occasionally. The school psychologist is responsible for testing, data collection, academic or learning interventions, and behavioral interventions. The school psychologist should be available for consultation and should usually attend support meetings.

- **The Principal** is usually who you go to if you are unhappy with how the teacher or school is handling your child's case. If the teacher doesn't recommend your child for testing, you can write a letter requesting testing to your principal, as described below.

- Your district's **Special Education Coordinator or Director** (sometimes called special services) is responsible for special education support throughout the district. If you need to escalate an issue above a principal, you can first speak with the Special Education Coordinator, and then the Superintendent of Education for your school district.

Your district may have other ways to support children, as described in the "RTI" section of Chapter 6. This might include a whole team providing services or aid. But unlike all other support options, an IEP plan contains a list of goals that a school district, by law, needs to fulfill. And progress on those goals is measured every year, as part of the IEP. This accountability is very powerful.

See "Finding Resources and Help," in Chapter 6, for advice on developing goals and a strategy, and good information sources. The www.fineuntilkindergarten.com website also has a list of information resources for every state.

Request Testing to Start the IEP Process

By law, you can write a letter to the school principal, requesting that your child be tested for an LD *at any time* after noticing symptoms of trouble learning. A parent, teacher, or service provider can refer a child for assessment.

Requesting testing is separate from anything that the teacher is currently trying in the classroom. You don't have to go through or ask permission from the teacher to request testing. Your request can be in addition to any efforts that the teacher or school are currently making.

In your letter, use the phrase: "I am writing to request that [your child's name] be given a full psycho-educational evaluation, and be evaluated for services under the Child Find obligations of the Individuals with Disabilities Education Act (IDEA.)" A sample letter with this sentence is in Appendix E, "Sample Letters."

When the principal receives your letter requesting LD testing, a *legal process* begins. From this point on, everything that the school does in response to you is dictated by the IDEA law, although states can set their own timeframes.

Because requesting testing is a legal procedure, you should include evidence that your child has an LD in order for the school to agree to test your child. You should also include evidence that the teacher has tried several different approaches and they haven't worked. For information on collecting evidence, see "Managing Information and Efforts" in Chapter 3, "Your Journey," and "Before You Claim Support: Gather Information from the Teacher," in Chapter 4, "Helping Your Child Succeed in School."

The IDEA law provides a Parent Training and Information Center (PTI) in every state,[78] and Parent Center (www.parentcenter.hub) provides an interactive map to find the PTI associated with your state.[79] It's a good idea to check with the PTI in your state, or with your state's Division of Special Education to see if there are changes in the timeframe. Understood.org has a good overview of the process and many tips for parents.[80] "Finding Resources and Help," in Chapter 6, lists books that can help.

What Happens During the IEP Process?

The *Basic Process for Claiming an IEP* diagram, shown below, shows how the application process works if there are no disagreements, and if you just apply and get an IEP.

The "Disagreeing with the School or System" section, below, talks about where in the process you and the school can disagree, and what you can do.

Basic Process for Claiming an IEP

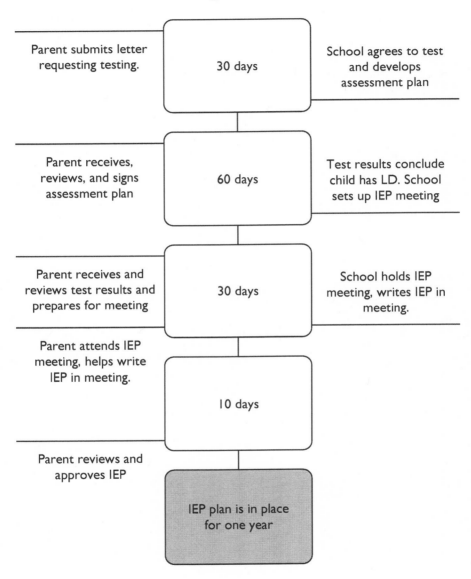

Parent submits letter requesting testing.

30 days

School agrees to test and develops assessment plan

Parent receives, reviews, and signs assessment plan

60 days

Test results conclude child has LD. School sets up IEP meeting

Parent receives and reviews test results and prepares for meeting

30 days

School holds IEP meeting, writes IEP in meeting.

Parent attends IEP meeting, helps write IEP in meeting.

10 days

Parent reviews and approves IEP

IEP plan is in place for one year

- **To start the process, you write and submit a letter requesting LD testing**

  - *The school district has 15 calendar days to consider your written request. If they refuse to test your child, they must send you a written notice, describing why.[81] (See "Disagreeing with the School and System" if they refuse.)*

  - *If the school agrees to test your child, they must develop an assessment plan and give it to you to review, within 15 more days.*

- **You receive, review, and sign the assessment plan:** If the school district agrees to test your child, they will present you with an Assessment Plan for your consent. When you receive an assessment plan, you have 15 days to ask questions and sign it.

  It's important that the school does a comprehensive evaluation, and identifies specific points where your child's learning process breaks down and how that impacts his classroom learning.[82] It is important that you review the assessment plan to make sure that the school is testing everything that they should. (See "Educational Testing and Claiming Support," below, and Appendix C, "The Whole-Child Diagnostic Approach.") When you have checked and approve, sign the assessment plan. The school will not test unless you sign.

  - *Once you sign the plan, the school must complete testing and conclude whether or not your child has LD within 60 days.*

  - *If the school determines that your child has a type of LD that is eligible for an IEP, the school schedules an IEP meeting to occur within 30 days.*

  - *The school should send you a copy of the test results before the IEP meeting. The school must also explain the test results to you before the IEP meeting.*

  - *If the school determines that your child doesn't have an LD that lets him qualify for an IEP, they will sometimes offer a 504 instead. (See "Claiming 504 Plan Support.")*

- **You receive and review test results before the IEP meeting:** If your child qualifies for an IEP, you are entitled to have the person who administered the test explain the test results to you before the IEP meeting. If your child is turned down for an IEP, or if the test results don't correctly reflect your child's challenges, then you should request an Independent Educational Evaluation, as described in "Disagreeing With the School and System," below.)

- **You research and prepare to be a participant in the IEP meeting**: Educate yourself about the IEP process and reach out for support. If you see problems that testing hasn't identified, bring them to the meeting. When the team sets up a meeting, they will establish education goals and objectives for your child, for this coming year.[83] Write down all of your input for the IEP so that it will be in the record.

- The school *holds an IEP meeting*, in which the IEP is written by an IEP team. **You are part of the IEP team, and participate in all meetings, discussion, and decisions.**[84] The meeting must contain people who can make decisions about how to support your child.[85]

Educational Testing and Claiming Support

Children with LD typically have multiple weaknesses that overlap,[86] so we suggest that you request a full educational evaluation, instead of just testing for one skill.

If the school district gives your child a full educational examination, they test up to seven areas of development:

- Language
- Visual and spatial thinking (also called nonverbal processing)
- Attention and self-regulation
- Memory
- Fine and gross motor skills
- Social and emotional abilities
- Executive function

Parents caution that just requesting a full educational evaluation doesn't guarantee that your child will get one. Make sure that you compare the test plan to the list above, and ask questions. You should request assistive technology testing[87] at the same time. Your child might need assistive technology includes keyboards, iPads, and other tools that compensate for disabilities.[88]

If you want the school district to add more types of testing to their testing plan, you might say "My child doesn't remember how to add, no matter how many times it is explained, so I want tests that specifically test his ability to understand numbers, to memorize things, and to write numbers." Being respectful, having good reasons behind your requests, and writing everything down are good ways to get what you want.

Some parents report that that in addition to requesting a full educational evaluation and an assistive technology test, they had to specify OT diagnostic testing, speech and auditory, and dyslexia testing. It's a good idea to write down what tests you want, and email them to the person in charge of testing. A paper trail is good.

In general, you should request that a pediatric occupational therapist be the person giving your child an evaluation. A pediatric OT understands the developmental steps, and will give a broader view than an OT who doesn't focus on pediatrics. For more information on developmental steps, see Chapter 7, "What They Don't Tell You About Learning Differences."

"The Whole-Child Diagnostic Approach," in Appendix C, can help you understand what other parents have tested, and why. And Appendix A, "What's Inside Your Child's Diagnosis?" shows weaknesses that are measured as part of every diagnosis. You can request that the school test for particular weaknesses.

Results of IEP Testing

The school district uses the results of your child's testing to determine if your child has an LD, and if your child qualifies for an IEP.[89]

An entire industry of legal fighting and arguing exists over the question of whether or not specific children qualify for IEPs. Just having a learning disability doesn't qualify a child for an IEP. Your child must qualify for two things in order to receive an IEP: Testing must conclude that your child is diagnosed with one of the 13 disabilities that are supported by IDEA.[90] Testing must also conclude that the disability adversely affects educational performance, and because of that, your child is unable to receive proper education.

Most of the learning differences that we mention in this book are covered by Specific Learning Differences category within IDEA.[91]

If you are told that your child does not qualify, and you disagree, you can request outside testing as described in "IEP Disagreements," below. If your child is turned down for an IEP and you don't want to disagree with the results of testing, you can request a 504 plan. The qualifications for getting a 504 are substantially easier than for getting an IEP. See "Qualifying for a 504," below.

Getting Support for ADHD: 504 and More

Many people think that their ADHD child is only eligible for support under Section 504, but this isn't true. IDEA provides support for ADHD children under the "other health impairment" category, the specific learning disability category, or the emotional disturbance category.[92] IDEA qualification means that ADHD children can be covered by an IEP.

What Should You Know About an IEP Meeting?

You should receive your child's test results and have them explained to you before the IEP meeting. Remember: all support is tied to test results. Also before the IEP meeting, both you and the district should research what will go into the IEP.[93]

When you attend an IEP meeting, the actions are scripted. You and the team show up, you need to do a certain number of things and produce certain output. There are thousands of websites and hundreds of books and pamphlets telling you how to attend an IEP meeting and what to do.

When you and the team develop an IEP, it will include the following:

- Your child's *present levels of achievement and performance*. Make sure that important information is in here. Don't let anything get dropped.

- A *statement of measurable goals*. This is important because these are legal goals. The school must meet them

- *Appropriate, measurable goals and benchmarks*. Any goals in the IEP should be written in measurable language (improves 30% or increases to the beginning of third grade level.)

- Specification of *scientifically-based instruction, provided by a qualified individual* (one with a special education teaching credential.)[94]

Consumers are encouraged to set up a SMART IEP. The SMART acronym refers to IEP goals, which should be: Specific, Measurable, using Action words, Realistic and relevant, and Time-limited.[95]

Here are the top tips from parents about succeeding in an IEP meeting:

- **Follow your gut** and don't back down. You know your child best.

- **Represent your child's needs**. When you attend an IEP meeting, you should bring with you all of the information that you have about your child, including his strengths, what motivates him, and what's the most effective way to teach him. Chapter 4, "Understanding Your Child" can help you to develop that information. Make sure that you have gone over test results with the people who tested, and that you have fully researched what all of the test results mean.

- **Come to the table with ideas or a proposal and ask for what you want**. Don't sit passively. Before the meeting, do your homework, talking with parents and experts to find out what options might be available for your child.

- **Know roughly what the school district is able to do for your child**. This is more homework. Become a detective. Find out how the school supports other children, and try to find names of good teachers and special education teachers in your district.

- **Consider bringing a friend or professional**. Many parents bring a good friend or someone who really knows the process. This is allowed.

- **Learn to aggressively request support technology**. If your child has trouble with math, handwriting, and reading, tools can absolutely change his world. Get those tools into the IEP (or 504 accommodations), and make sure that teachers are trained in how to work with a child who uses those tools. For memory issues, consider letting your child take pictures of the white board. The Fine Until Kindergarten website has lists of support technology.

- **Request 24 hours in advance that you be able to tape record the meeting**. On the day of the meeting, keep it light. Make a joke about poor memory and thank them for letting you record. Anything to keep things friendly, while at the same time exercising your legal rights.

- **Don't sign anything** the day of the meeting. We all need to think things over.

- **You can always call another meeting**! Parents report calling another meeting if:

  ◦ *A person who can make decisions about your child's education isn't present at the meeting (they must attend, by law).*

  ◦ *Anybody who should be at the meeting missing.*

  ◦ *The IEP isn't completed at the meeting.*

  ◦ *Parents cannot come to agreement with the district at the meeting.*

In addition, parents report that the way in which schools describe your child in these meetings is relentlessly negative—be prepared for it.

The best book for parents just starting to work on claiming either 504 plan or IEP support is *From Emotion to Advocacy*, by Pam and Pete Wright. The Wrightslaw website contains many articles and tips for how to put together an IEP.[96] It even contains an excerpt from their book, talking about how to write a SMART IEP.[97]

Claiming 504 Plan Support

A 504 plan can provide for accommodations, modifications, and support for your child. It's commonly used to provide things like more time, the ability to type papers instead of handwrite them, or having a teacher read the test. In general, the 504 plan doesn't include services like OT, although the law allows for it.

A 504 plan also includes the names of professionals who will provide the support. One person is responsible for making sure that the 504 plan is implemented.

To qualify for a 504, your child must have a disability that interferes with her major life activities, which includes reading and concentrating, and ability to learn or access school programs. Learning and attention issues often fall into this category.[98]

Often, if a child is tested for an IEP and doesn't qualify, the child will be offered a 504 as a kind of "consolation prize." While a 504 might provide valuable help, if you strongly believe that your child should qualify for an IEP, parents strongly suggest that you keep fighting.

Most experts counsel parents to strongly consider applying for an IEP if their child's disability in any way falls within the qualifications. While some districts will easily give out a 504 plan, other districts will not, and the 504 process doesn't include any goals that the school must meet in educating your child. It also doesn't include the protections provided by the IEP process.

The most straightforward way to request a 504 plan is to write a letter requesting a 504 and give it to the principal. In the letter, include descriptions of the problems that your child has learning, and any diagnoses that you have. Include the words: "I request a 504 plan for my child." See the letters in Appendix E for how to give examples of your child's learning disability. After receiving the letter, the school calls a 504 meeting. When you attend the 504 meeting, you can bring examples of your child's work. Unlike the IEP meetings, where you must attend, the law doesn't require or guarantee your attendance at 504 meetings.

Each district may have a different process for applying for a 504, so it's a good idea to go to your school district's website and see if there are specific directions.

For more information about accommodations, see "Working with Accommodations," in Chapter 4, "Helping Your Child Succeed in School."

Disagreeing with the School and System

When you request support for your child, it's a little bit like filling out forms at the DMV. There is a set of options within the law. One of the things that you may do—as specified by the IDEA law—is to formally disagree with how the school handles your child's case.

When Can Disagreements Happen in the IEP Process?

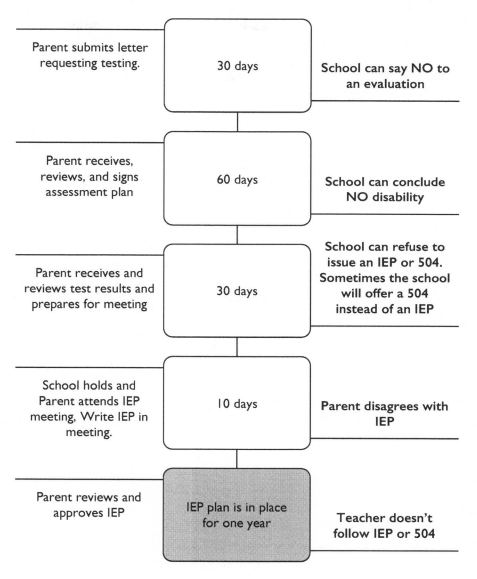

Parent submits letter requesting testing.	30 days	**School can say NO to an evaluation**
Parent receives, reviews, and signs assessment plan	60 days	**School can conclude NO disability**
Parent receives and reviews test results and prepares for meeting	30 days	**School can refuse to issue an IEP or 504. Sometimes the school will offer a 504 instead of an IEP**
School holds and Parent attends IEP meeting, Write IEP in meeting.	10 days	**Parent disagrees with IEP**
Parent reviews and approves IEP	IEP plan is in place for one year	**Teacher doesn't follow IEP or 504**

Don't be too intimidated to file a due process complaint, if necessary. You can do this!

Here are five example points on which parents can disagree with what is going on when they try to claim support:

Refuse to Test Child

The law requires the school to evaluate children for LD.[99]

If you request a formal evaluation in writing, the school district evaluates your information. If they find no proof of an LD, they can say **NO to an evaluation**.

If the school district refuses to test your child, they must send you a letter within 10 days, telling you why, and on what they based their decision. If you don't understand or accept their reason, go ahead and call a meeting to discuss your concerns. You can ask for details and data about why they feel that your child doesn't have a disability. Remember to bring your own data to the meeting. If they still refuse to evaluate at the end of the meeting, ask for information on your legal rights. The letter you received from the school district contains additional directions for how to disagree within your school district.

In some cases, you can ask for an Independent Educational Evaluation, in which the school pays to have an outside professional test your child. (See below.) You can also have your child evaluated by outside testing professionals, and pay yourself, and then write a letter requesting an IEP, saying that you have outside testing results.

School Denies LD After Testing:

The school can agree to test, but after testing, the testing team can conclude that your child has **NO disability**. If the school denies support to your child, it must send you a letter explaining why, and what tests were used. With that letter is a letter explaining what you can do in the process. If you don't understand the school's explanation you have the legal right to request that they explain it to you. A big question in this type of case is whether or not the school tested correctly. Sometimes your child can qualify for support through more than one category.

Asking for an Independent Educational Evaluation (IEE)

When the district explains your child's test results to you, if you feel that the test results don't accurately represent your child's learning needs, you have the right to have your child evaluated by a medical doctor and/or outside educational specialist. This is called an *independent educational evaluation* (IEE). In some cases, the school district will agree to pay for the IEE. Two other reasons why parents request an Independent Educational Evaluation (IEE), include:

- The evaluation wasn't done in your child's native language.
- You feel that the original evaluation was incomplete and additional tests are needed.

You can request that the school district pay for the IEE by writing a letter before an outside evaluation, and sending it to the special education coordinator or principal at your child's school. It's a good idea to send the letter "return receipt requested" from the post office, so you have proof that it was received. In your letter, state your child's name, when she was evaluated, why you feel that the evaluation wasn't complete, and describe specifically what types of tests you want.[100]

When you request that the school pay for an IEE, your district will set up a hearing. A hearing officer will preside over the hearing and will decide whether the school will pay for an independent evaluation. If the hearing officer decides against your request, you can still get an independent evaluation, but you will have to pay for it.

If you get an IEE, the IEP team must take the IEE results into consideration when evaluating your IEP request. In addition to hiring your own testing professional, you you can read books, take classes, and hire advocates to work with you in the IEP process. For more information, see "Finding Resources and Help" in Chapter 6, "School Support Programs for LD."

Doesn't Qualify for IEP

The school can determine that, even though your child has an LD, he doesn't qualify for an IEP. In this case they will **refuse to issue an IEP**. Sometimes, they will give a 504 instead.[101] You can disagree with this. In this case, you need to research the law and your case, and perhaps bring in an advocate. See "Finding Resources and Help" in Chapter 6.

IEP Doesn't Support Needs

The IEP team can refuse to support your child's needs by providing an incomplete IEP. (This is shown as **"Parent disagrees with the contents of IEP.**)

If you are unhappy with the IEP that the team comes up with during the IEP meeting, you can refuse to sign it. However, most parents suggest that you sign it, but mark that you only agree with part of it. This will ensure that the school begins supporting your child while you continue to negotiate.

A good thing to do in this situation is to request another IEP meeting, then take classes and read books before the meeting. The Wrightslaw.com website can help with specific questions. You also might want to consider hiring an advocate.

Teacher isn't Following IEP

Sometimes a teacher or school **refuses to follow the IEP**.

The Wrightslaw website describes a process to follow if your child's IEP isn't being followed.[102] First, write to the principal and schedule a discussion. Then, the Special Education Director. After that, the Superintendent and school board members. If the problem continues, you can request a due process hearing or file a complaint with the Office of Civil Rights.

Filing a Due Process Complaint

If you feel that the school district is violating IDEA by not declaring your child eligible for an IEP, by not providing an IEP that supports your child's needs, or by not following and enforcing your child's IEP, you can submit a *due process complaint*. There are fewer than 50 mediation requests per 10,000 special education students, so few parents take advantage of this part of the law.[103] Don't be intimidated. If you feel that you're not being supported, the law supports the filing of due process complaints.

A due process complaint, also called a "hearing request," is a written document that can be filed by a parent or a school district. This starts a process that may lead to a formal hearing where a hearing officer decides the outcome. A parent doesn't need an attorney to file a due process complaint, although parents may choose to hire one.

The Wrightslaw website offers a DVD called "Surviving Due Process: Stephen Jeffers v. School Board." The DVD takes you though a special education due process hearing from initial preparations to testimony by the final witness. The film is based upon an actual case.[104]

The Wrightslaw website also offers a download of instructions for writing a due process request letter or a state complaint.[105]

Due process complaints differ by state. Details on how to file a due process complaint for your state are available from your state's State Educational Agency (SEA).[106] In general, IDEA requires that a due process complaint include:

- Name of child and name of child's school
- A description of the specific problem and facts to support the description.
- Ideas or suggestions to solve the problem.

The parent must send a copy of the Due Process complaint to the school district at the same time as they file the complaint with the SEA.

The SEA will send a letter to you and the school district with information about what you can expect to happen. This letter will include:

- Name and contact information of your hearing officer.
- Due process timelines.
- Information about mediation.
- Information about legal resources.

The school district has 10 calendar days to respond, and the district must schedule a meeting within 15 days of receiving the complaint, unless you and the district agree in writing to use mediation, or not to have a resolution meeting.

If a due process hearing takes place, the hearing office must mail a copy of the decision to each party no longer than 45 calendar days from the beginning of the hearing timeline.

The hearing officer's decision is legally binding, even if you disagree with the outcome, unless the decision is appealed.

Clashing with the School

LD parent groups and internet forums are full of parents who will tell you depressing stories of being treated unfairly and poorly by their school districts. Claiming support for disabled students is an old fight, and one which has gone through many rounds. In the endnotes for this chapter, you'll see several letters from the US Department of education to school districts, telling them to support various issues, but the fact is: many school districts will try hard to not give your child an IEP.

In this chapter, we walked you through the basic process, but in reality, the process can be a full battle. Law is always up to interpretation, and many school districts just deny that they need to support various LDs. If you run into this type of situation, you'll need to pull back, learn the law, and treat the situation like a lawsuit. But don't stop. The world is also full of parents who are using their school and retirement funds to pay for their LD child's education. Before you go there, try hard to claim benefits.

Chapter 6 describes how to learn more about the IEP process and how to hire professionals to help. But it's best to look for other parents who have been through the process and can give you advice.

If you need to go up against your school to get support for your child, make sure that you read the law yourself, even if you hire a professional to help. The Wrightslaw website[107] contains a page of resources that can help you learn.

CHAPTER 6:
School Support Programs for LD

If a child can't learn the way we teach, maybe we should teach the way they learn.

—*Ignacio Estrada*

We talk about school support programs throughout this book, and in this chapter we describe both the 504 plan and and the IEP. This chapter describes the laws that provide for both the IEP and 504 plan, explains how both programs work, and talks about benefits and disadvantages of both. In addition, we describe the Response to Intervention program, a school-based support program that doesn't require testing.

Even before your child enters school, federal laws and grants provide access to services and support.[108]

What Are the Laws?

Two laws are always mentioned when people talk about getting support from the educational system:

- **Section 504** of the Rehabilitation Act of 1973 is a civil rights law that protects people with disabilities from discrimination. Section 504 ensures that a child with a disability has equal access to education, and provides accommodations and/or modifications to normal schoolwork. [109] Section 504 defines "disability" broadly, and can help children with learning and attention issues succeed in a general education classroom.[110]

  When your child qualifies for services under this act, your child is said to *have a 504 plan*. A 504 plan is often used for children who need more time on tests, hearing support, scribing help (taking dictation), a keyboard, or other accommodations. For more information on 504 plans, including benefits and disadvantages, see "504 Plan," below.

- **IDEA** is the Individuals with Disabilities Education Act, which was enacted by Congress in 1975 to ensure that all children have the opportunity to receive a free and appropriate public education, regardless of ability. IDEA provides for most of the protection for children with LD, and laws in IDEA spell out the basic tool of special education: the *Independent Education Plan,* or *IEP*.

  When your child qualifies for services under this act, your child is said to *have an IEP*. IEPs are supported by the special education department, and typically, children with an IEP require at least some support from a teacher with a special education credential. For more information, including benefits and disadvantages, see "IEP," below.

- In addition to the two laws that provide support for children, schools are allowed to use some of their IDEA funding to set up early educational interventions within a school's general programs. This is called a **Response to Intervention (RTI)** program. Students don't need a diagnosis to qualify for an RTI intervention. Typically, RTI services are provided by general-education teachers. For more information on the RTI program, see "Response to Intervention," below.

Parents do not have to pay to request or receive 504, IEP, or RTI services for their child.

Response to Intervention

Your child can be put into a RTI program at any time, without waiting to be tested. It's simply another way of supporting education. In 2006, many states began to use a RTI approach for children who were having academic trouble. The RTI was developed because the federal government wanted teachers to be able to flag children to get learning support before being tested for an LD.[111] The federal government allows school districts to use up to 15% of their IDEA funding to pay for the RTI early intervention program. (In some states, it has different names and different rules.)

RTI offers an alternative to putting children who are having trouble in school through special-needs testing. With the RTI program, teachers identify students who have problems, and then, while keeping them in the classroom, use different teaching techniques.[112] Teachers track patterns of strengths and weaknesses,[113] to see if the new techniques work.[114] There are multiple tiers of intervention. If a child is involved in RTI and doesn't improve, then eventually the school will test that child, but there is no guarantee when that will happen.

The National Center for Learning Disabilities has a free, downloadable e-book called "A Parent's Guide to RTI.[115]

Since the 1970's, students identified with specific learning disabilities increased 200%.[116] Specific learning disabilities include dyslexia, the ability to understand or use language, write, listen, read, spell, or do math. Since the government has started using the RTI program, the number of children formally identified with specific learning disabilities has reduced, allowing districts to hire fewer special-needs teachers.[117]

Benefits of RTI

Originally, RTI was defined as student-centered assessment models that use problem-solving and research-based methods. It has also been described as a way for districts to provide interventions as soon as a need arises, without having to wait for the child to fail.

Some school districts use RTI in addition to other interventions, as a structured way to support learning. It can be very helpful to have a structured alternative program available to children who are having trouble. RTI allows schools to identify students with problems early, support them, and test theories for why the child is failing.

Disadvantages of RTI

Unlike other plans, districts are not legally obligated to follow through on RTI suggestions or structure. An RTI is even less binding than a 504 plan. Since there's no legal guarantee that teachers will appropriately follow an RTI plan, stay vigilant if you agree to one.

Many parents of students with learning disabilities feel their children were delayed from getting special education testing and services they needed because they agreed to RTI.[118] Likewise, some school employees have said that they felt that RTI kept students from getting appropriate special education help. And some teachers have expressed frustration with RTI, saying it requires teachers without special education training to provide special education teaching.

An article published in Information Week in 2015, talks about how RTI is falling short of its promise. The article, written by Sarah Sparks, cites a study with more than 20,000 students in 13 states. In addition to other findings, the report discovered that students who were already in special education, or who were old for their grade, performed poorly when they received RTI.

Douglas Fuchs, a professor and chair of special education and human development at Vanderbilt University, says that "over time, in many places, what's happened is RTI has been deliberately used as a kind of general education substitution for special education."[119]

Take-away? Parents suggest that if you feel your child really needs a special education support plan, don't settle for an RTI. Legally, you don't have to go with RTI, and information from an RTI is not needed in order to test for learning differences. Remember: you can write a letter asking for testing, *even if you've already agreed to an RTI.* If your school district tries to make you send your child to RTI instead of getting tested,

- write your letter requesting testing, as shown in Appendix E, and then

- print out and attach the 2011 letter from the United States Department of Education, which forbids using RTI to delay testing (link is on page in endnote).[120]

- If your school district still refuses to test your child, request that they put the refusal in writing. Since they are breaking the law, asking schools to write this type of thing down often results in the school doing the right thing. And you can take a written refusal and complain, as described in "Disagreeing with the School and System," in Chapter 5, "Claiming Support in the School System."

504 Plan

Section 504 of the Rehabilitation Act was passed in 1973 to prohibit discrimination based on ability. It's a sweeping civil rights law, and part of section 504 is devoted to providing access to education for children with disabilities. In schools, a 504 plan makes sure that children with learning disabilities can participate in school without discrimination.

In order for your child to qualify for a 504, a student must have documentation from a doctor proving that he has a non-temporary physical or mental impairment that limits one or more major life activity. This can include reading, writing, concentrating, or more. Although children still need to qualify for a 504, the definition is broader than an IEP and more children qualify for a 504. Often, if a child has ADHD or mild dyslexia, but doesn't need an IEP, he will qualify for a 504 instead.

Typically, a 504 plan contains a list of *accommodations* that a teacher must either provide, or allow a student with a disability to use in the classroom. An accommodation alters the academic setting or environment in some way, but doesn't change the content of required work. The 504 accommodations remove obstacles that keep children from learning.

- Language disorder accommodations may include listening to books on tape, instead of reading.

- Writing disorder accommodations may include letting your child use a scribe (a person who writes things down), or a keyboard, instead of hand-writing everything.

- Auditory processing disorder accommodations may include allowing a child to wear an FM device so that she can hear better.

When you list accommodations in a 504 plan, your child's access to these accommodations is protected by law.

There is no limit to the number of accommodations that can be listed on a 504. It's a good idea, though, to choose a list that is easy to understand and can be easily communicated to teachers, and enforced. If you move from a 504 to an IEP, you can move your list of accommodations into the IEP. For more information on accommodations, see "Working with Accommodations and Modifications," in Chapter 4, "Helping Your Child Succeed in School."

A 504 plan can also include *modifications*, which allow a student to complete an assignment, but simplify or change the quantity or skill level of the work required. An example modification is fewer math or spelling questions, different questions, shorter writing assignments, and teacher-provided notes or study guides.

To get a 504 plan, a parent provides an evaluation to a 504 team, which includes the child's teacher, a special education teacher, the school principal. Although a parent's involvement in this meeting isn't guaranteed by law, you can ask to attend. A 504 plan needs to be renewed every year.

Who is Eligible for a 504?

If a child has an LD or disability but doesn't need or qualify for special education services (an IEP), they might qualify for a 504. Section 504 specifies that a child who is limited in major life activities, which include "seeing, hearing, learning, reading, writing, performing math calculations, and performing manual tasks," is eligible for a 504.

Benefits of a 504

Accommodations are relatively simple for school districts to provide, and they cost nothing. Because of this, and the broad requirements for qualifying, it's easier to qualify for a 504 than an IEP. Since the 504 accommodations are protected by law, you can follow up and complain if they are not followed. By listing your child's accommodations (and perhaps writing a letter to the teacher at the start of a school year,) you can make it very clear what will help your child to succeed.

Some of the common ways in which children can benefit from a 504 include:

- Reduced workload or number of problems means that a slower-working or different-learning child can focus on how to do the work, instead of trying to complete large numbers of problems.

- Hearing, reading, and other input accommodations can mean the difference between understanding and becoming overwhelmed.

- Processing speed accommodations, like extra time on tests and assignments, can mean the difference between doing well and flunking.

- Memory aid accommodations can save your child frustrating years of trying to memorize math (for example), or even days of the week.

- Output accommodations, like a scribe, a keyboard, or learning how to use dictation software can mean the difference between your child spending hours to write something incomprehensible, versus your child working to develop real writing skills and being able to focus on what is being taught.

Disadvantages of a 504

Unlike an IEP, section 504 doesn't ensure that a child with a disability will receive any sort of individualized education. There are no educational goals associated with a 504, and rarely will teachers modify the content of a course with a 504. Section 504 doesn't require a teacher to teach things differently.

Many teachers use a 504 to require less work from children (for example, 3 spelling words instead of 15). Unfortunately, while this might lessen the homework burden, it doesn't teach the child. Because of this, some parents state that their child's 504 was just used to "fail their child forward," passing them to the next grade without learning what was necessary. It is important to make sure that your child's type of learning is supported by the teacher. If your child is not able to learn in the classroom, it's time to talk with the principal, and possibly request an IEP.

There is no standardized teacher training for dealing with 504 accommodations. Different teachers support a 504 differently, and parents sometimes have to work hard to make sure that their child's 504 is followed. Some teachers refuse to follow a 504.

Individualized Education Program

The IEP is a plan for a child's entire experience within a school. It contains specific measurable goals, and is an important legal document that both protects and opens the door to educational, social, and behavioral support for disabilities. In order to qualify for an IEP, your child must be tested and diagnosed for a learning disability that is listed in the IDEA, as described in Chapter 5.

Understanding the IEP information can be overwhelming, since many IEP websites are full of complex information. The website Understood.org has worked hard to present IEP information in small chunks,[121], with an introduction to Individualized Education Programs,[122] and a description of the process of getting an IEP.[123]

If your child has been granted an IEP, you'll want to touch base with the teacher at the start of the year, to make sure that he or she understands the IEP. You'll also want to pay attention throughout the school year, making sure that the IEP is followed.

Every IEP requires a yearly meeting of the school's IEP team. The basic team must include at least one regular education teacher, at least one special education teacher, a representative from the school district who has power to make decisions about your child's education, and you. The meeting might also include the special education director, the principal, and any experts you choose to invite. The yearly meeting discusses whether or not goals were met from the previous year, whether your child will have an IEP this coming year, and what will be in the IEP. If you have concerns, bring them to the meeting, together with examples.

Although this is only an overview of the IEP, there are a few things that should be repeated for parents, again and again:

You can call an IEP meeting at any time. If you don't understand or are feeling rushed, you can always request another meeting. This is provided for by law.

Don't ever let anybody push you into signing something in an IEP meeting. It's a good policy, actually, to just say that you need to "sleep on it" or you need to show the IEP to someone, so that you aren't pressured into signing an IEP. Then go home and really study it.

Who Is Eligible for an IEP?

Qualifying for the IEP requires two things. First off, your child must be diagnosed with a condition that is covered by the Individuals with Disabilities Education Act (IDEA)." There are 13 disabilities listed in the IDEA.[124] Most children with learning differences potentially qualify under the *specific learning disability* category. Children with ADHD potentially qualify under a category called *other health impairment*.

IDEA defines specific learning disability as: "a disorder in one or more of the basic psychological processes involved in understanding or in using language, spoken or written, that may manifest itself in the im-

105

perfect ability to listen, think, speak, read, write, spell, or to do mathematical calculations. The term includes such conditions as perceptual disabilities, brain injury, minimal brain dysfunction, dyslexia, and developmental aphasia. The term does not include learning problems that are primarily the result of visual, hearing, or motor disabilities; of intellectual disability; of emotional disturbance; or of environmental, cultural, or economic disadvantage."

Secondly, in order to qualify for an IEP, you must prove that your child's disability prevents him or her from receiving an education, and that your child needs services in order to progress in school. In other words, your child must need something that the school doesn't offer as part of its regular program.

Getting an IEP might seem straightforward, but in many school districts, especially for disorders like ADHD, dyslexia, dysgraphia, and auditory processing disorder, parents report that it's very difficult to get an IEP. Many school districts tell parents that "you cannot get an IEP for dyslexia *despite the fact that dyslexia is listed in the law*!" The way to do it, say the parents who have gotten an IEP, is to throw yourself into it. Read the law. Read books about how to get an IEP. Talk to other parents. And then do it, one foot after the other. See also "Finding Resources and Help," below.

What Does an IEP Do?

An IEP is an individual plan that ensures curriculum in general classrooms is flexible enough to support your child's learning, and provides services as needed. An IEP can also specify education outside of the general classroom. An IEP is a legally binding document. It must include the following:

- A **statement** on how your child is currently doing, and on how your child's disability affects learning and life.

- A list of your child's annual educational **goals**, which can include behavioral and social goals

- A **description** of the special education supports and services that the school will provide to help reach goals in the IEP, including when services will begin, how often, where, and how long they will last.

- **Descriptions** of program and test modifications and classroom accommodations the school will provide,
- If there was previously a 504, it can be included in the IEP.
- **Plans** for measuring progress toward annual goals

If your child has an IEP, he may be eligible for support products purchased as part of the IEP.

Benefits of an IEP

An IEP is federally mandated and comes with full protection of the law. Each IEP has specific, customized goals attached to it every year that target your child's particular needs, and there are consequences if the goals are not met.

The IEP process is built around protecting and informing the parent. If a parent has problems or disagrees, there are clearly-defined ways to lodge a complaint and request change. See "Disagreeing with the School and System" in Chapter 5, "Claiming Support in the School System."

Disadvantages of an IEP

There's no disadvantage to having an IEP, although many parents whose children have IEPs report having problems with how school districts interpret and support the IEP. District resources may be limited and problems may vary, depending on how willing educators are to create an effective, personalized learning environment.

Finding Resources and Help

There are many places to find help. Although the laws setting up special education are federal, each state can have different dates and rules for claiming support. It's a good idea to start by reading the simple instructions that have been written for parents in your state. The www.fineuntilkindergarten.com website has a document listing Special Education resources, by state.[125]

The IEP process is a complex, legal process, but like many legal processes, it seems a lot more complex than it needs to be. Furthermore, many of the people who explain IEP laws to parents don't make it as simple as they could. For this reason, parents suggest that you learn about the IEP process from three sources, at the same time:

Other Parents

The most important thing to know in any legal situation is: what should you want, and how do you get it, in the most effective fashion. If you have the opportunity, ask a parent! Parents can tell you what you need to know, who the resources are, and what works. Furthermore, parents can tell you how their situation was handled.

Even if you're an introvert, ask for help in finding parents who have been through this process. Ask the president of the PTA, ask local doctors, ask the counselor, ask teachers. Ask on the internet. (See also "The Power of Community: Joining Support Groups," in Chapter 3.)

There is no set way for parents to find one another. This means that it's hard for parents to share information and be effective. One of our goals at *Fine Until Kindergarten* is to fix this. Please sign up at the *Fine Until Kindergarten* website[126]—join our Reader's List!—and we will share information as we gather and distribute it.

Finally, remember that you can either hire an advocate, as described in "Hiring Professionals to Help," below, or you can just ask a friend to attend the IEP meeting with you. Parents who have been through the process are often very happy to reach out and help other families. Communication is key to success.

Books

There are some excellent books that you can read.

- In Chapter 5, we reference the book *From Emotion to Advocacy*, written by husband-wife lawyers Peter Wright and Pamela Wright. Pete Wright was diagnosed in second grade with learning disorders, including dyslexia, dysgraphia, and ADHD. His parents got intensive Orton-Gillingham remediation for him, and he studied both psychology and law. The Wrights have also written *All About IEPs* and *All About Tests and Assessments*.

- The Fine Until Kindergarten website lists more reference books for readers. See www.fineuntilkindergarten.com/bonus.

Websites

While websites are a wonderful resource, it's good to remember that each state can have their own legal variations, so it's good to find out what your state requires. To see resources that, by law, your state is required to provide, simply type the following into your internet search engine: State name IEP help. For example: Minnesota IEP help will return a list of help resources about getting an IEP in Minnesota.

- www.understood.org is a relatively new consortium of LD support organizations that delivers LD information to parents.

- The Wrightslaw website can be extremely intimidating to the first-time user, but if you get into a prolonged legal battle with your district, you will be very happy for it. The Wrightslaw website was created by the writers of the *From Emotion to Advocacy* book, described above.

- There are many other wonderful websites that contain information about IEPs and helping your child. You can search the internet for [your state name] IEP Advice to find state-specific information. In addition, almost every resource in the Endnotes section is one that you might find useful.

- The www.fineuntilkindergarten.com/bonus page contains links to every footnote in this book. In addition, it contains many bonus resources for *Fine Until Kindergarten* readers.

Hiring IEP Support Professionals

Some parents hire consultants who will help them get their information together and request an IEP.[127] The type of professionals who provide this type of service are called advocates, or IEP advocates. Some educational consultants are qualified to perform advocacy services, and some Attorneys at Law specialize in educational law and IEPs. Although you can use the internet to find this type of professional, it's much better to get a referral from another parent, since quality can vary.

If you are going to hire an advocate, it's perfectly acceptable to ask for (and check) parent references. You can also ask specifically for a referral from someone who has a case similar to yours. It's also a good idea to compare prices and negotiate cost.

Although an advocate can coach you on legal possibilities, it's best to think about what you want for your child before you interview or hire a professional. You can get an idea of what you might want from doing a bit of reading, and from talking with other parents. Sometimes a teacher will give you some pointers as well (off the record, usually.)

You can then approach an advocate or two, explain your child's learning profile and educational needs, and ask them what types of services they provide to help your child get the support that you would like. And then you can compare what two (or more) different advocates tell you. Be cautious and well-informed when you hire professionals to help. And remember: you can take anyone you wish to an IEP meeting. It can be your sister or a neighbor. It doesn't have to be a paid professional.

CHAPTER 7:
What They Don't Tell You About Learning Differences

The brain possesses a remarkable capacity to "re-wire" itself in response to experience. By carefully targeting inputs (through teaching, therapy, or play), existing brain pathways can be trained to function more smoothly, old blocks can be bypassed by new learning pathways, and children can master skills that they previously found impossible.

—Brock Eide, MD, Fernette Eide, MD *The Mislabeled Child*

A diagnosis doesn't automatically put your child on a path to success. Traditionally a doctor or specialist identifies learning challenges and assigns a diagnosis. It is then up to a different set of people: therapists, parents, and teachers, to help a child improve skills and learn.

Unfortunately, there's often a chasm between receiving a diagnosis and working with your child to help her develop and succeed.

Our doctors are taught their specialties in various silos. If you hurt your foot, you go to a podiatrist. If you have stomach trouble, you go to a gastroenterologist. While we may think that our pediatrician knows everything (and many are amazing), very few pediatricians or doctors specialize in learning issues. It's the parent's job to figure out what needs to be done to help their child, and then make sure it gets done.

This can be a difficult task, because parents must deal with several different doctors and therapists, in addition to teachers.

This chapter gives you a pragmatic overview to:

- Understanding your child's diagnosis, and what it tells you about potential growth areas,
- Learning what role brain maturity might play in your child's challenges, and
- Discovering how therapy might help.

From Diagnosis to Success: Working with Therapy Providers

We've already counseled you to start by claiming support from the educational system. Your child's school will often provide speech therapy, occupational therapy, handwriting therapy and sometimes more. But in this chapter, we'll also talk about hiring outside professionals. Since it's expensive to purchase therapy, we suggest that you get a diagnosis first, and then find out if your insurance company pays for any therapy. Sometimes, an insurance company will pay for speech therapy or occupational therapy.

Unfortunately, most other therapies are not paid for by insurance, so parents have to pay out of pocket. Therapy often costs $150 an hour, which can add up, fast. It is extremely important to check references and talk with other parents, so that you can ask questions about the therapy and the provider.

The "Working with Professionals" section of Chapter 3, "Your Journey," talks about how to interview therapists, set up a three-month working period, and set and check goals. Although not every therapist will do this, it's good to discuss your expectations at the beginning of sessions.

Many of the skills that hamper LD children are tied to brain maturity, and countless children with LDs of one sort or another have been helped by therapists: speech, vision, occupational (or other movement), and educational.

Books like *Smart Moves*, by Carla Hannaford, Ph.D., and *The Well Balanced Child: Movement and Early Learning*, by Sally Goddard Blythe, talk about the importance of brain maturity and learning. Books like *The Out-of-Sync Child* book series, by Carol Stock Kranowitz, M.A., and *Brain Gym*, by Dr. Paul Dennison, contain example activities and exercises that can help a child's brain mature.

It's difficult to find a doctor who works closely with parents to diagnose LDs, and then helps them select and manage therapy. One such doctor is Dr. Susan Johnson, M.D., FAAP. Dr. Johnson is an integrative diagnostic pediatrician, who has published a book called *Healing Our Children*, describing her clinical experiences and observations.

Therapists often receive their certifications, as described in Appendix D, "Types of Doctors and Specialists," and then continue specialized training for decades. This lets them be on the forefront of new knowledge about what helps children. Mary Scholer is an occupational therapist and Executive Director of the Simoneon Pediatric Development Center in San Jose, with over 35 years of experience and training. In her therapy sessions, Mary explains that she helps develop a child's physical, sensory, and motor development, laying the foundation for developing academic skills.

The skill that Mary and other OTs have is a specialized skill. Many doctors know nothing about the details of what an occupational therapist does. And very few teachers know, either. It's up to the parent to put all of the pieces together into a big picture.

What Should You Know About Your Child's Diagnosis?

In addition to helping your child qualify for a 504 plan or IEP, your child's LD diagnosis pinpoints his personal learning strengths and weaknesses. Once your child is diagnosed, you'll be able to do a better job supporting his development and learning.

When children are tested for LD, they are given a battery of tests that measure their cognitive skills and identify weaknesses. A cognitive skill can be simple, like recognizing phonics or remembering a list of numbers, or it can be complex, like the ability to organize. As shown in Appendix A, each diagnosis is made up of several cognitive weaknesses.

When you get the results of your child's diagnosis, the test results will show you both strengths and weaknesses. Weaknesses are typically skills needed for academic success.

You Can Think of a Diagnosis as an Umbrella

When a doctor evaluates your child's abilities, he is taking a snapshot of your child's development at this point in time. Your child will continue to develop and grow.

In Appendix A, "What's Inside Your Child's Diagnosis?" we show different diagnoses as umbrellas, and we list common *associated weaknesses* for each diagnosis underneath each umbrella. If your child has a diagnosis, she may display one or more of these weaknesses. Every child's profile is different.

When you discuss your child's diagnostic test results with your doctor, the figures in Appendix A let you check boxes next to any weaknesses. Your doctor can help you do this. The better you understand your child's strengths and weaknesses, the more you can make sure that her education supports her appropriately.

What's Inside of a Diagnostic Umbrella?

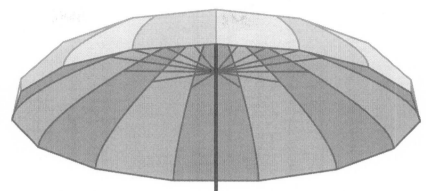

- Appendix A lists weaknesses associated with each diagnosis.

- Some children only have one or two weaknesses associated with a diagnosis.

- Learning more about your child's diagnosis helps your child succeed.

- We use "weaknesses," instead of "deficit," or "challenge," because some weaknesses can be strengthened.

Look at Your Child's Cognitive Weaknesses

A diagnosis can seem overwhelming, but when you break it down into a collection of cognitive weaknesses, you can start to address those weaknesses directly, either through targeted teaching, or through accommodations or therapies. A diagnosis can give us an idea of which brain systems

It's important to help schools to not just dwell on where your child falls short, but to also take your child's strengths into consideration. See "Creating and Using a Learning Profile," in Chapter 4, "Helping Your Child Succeed in School."

show weakness. Many cognitive weaknesses are caused by the following:

- Sometimes systems in the brain are **late to mature**.

  If some of your child's brain systems are late to mature, then therapy (often called pediatric occupational therapy, or OT) can help.

- Sometimes two or more systems in the brain **need to learn to work together**, or integrate.

  If two brain systems are maturing unevenly, or don't work together well, then therapy (again, often OT, but sometimes vision therapy, auditory integration therapy, or speech therapy) can help the systems integrate, or work together better. Sometimes therapy helps a bit, but doesn't get rid of the problem entirely. In this case, your child may end up having a brain that just works differently.

- Sometimes a brain system, or group of brain systems, **just work differently**.

  This is the classic definition of a learning disability. If a brain system just works differently, then it's like being left handed. We now know that a differently-working brain system carries with it some strengths, like seeing the big picture, creativity, and so forth.[128] But we also know that targeted early intervention programs that teach using different techniques can bring many LD kids back into mainstream, teaching children how to learn in our school system.[129] In these cases, the LD brain still works differently, but it has learned new skills and can cope with schoolwork.

Studies tell us that early intervention results in narrowing the achievement gap.[130] Therapies can also narrow the achievement gap, by helping brain systems to develop.

As adults, we strengthen and fine-tune our brains all the time. We take classes and practice memorizing things, we practice sports, we practice instruments. Some cognitive weaknesses respond well to therapy. Other cognitive weaknesses indicate that you should teach your child in a certain way in order to be effective. Studies are now beginning to show that cognitive training might also help to strengthen the brain.[131]

Pinning Down a Diagnosis Can Be Hard

When parents start learning about their child's learning challenges, it can be very confusing because of three issues:

- Since many learning differences share symptoms, cognitive skills, and brain systems, there's often not a clear border between different diagnoses.[132]

- Children are often diagnosed with more than one learning difference. This is called *comorbidity*. *Comorbidity is the rule with learning differences, rather than the exception.* 60% of children diagnosed with ADHD, and 50% of children diagnosed with dyslexia are also diagnosed with other disorders. [133]

- Neither the educational nor the medical professions use standard, agreed-upon testing terms or testing categories. It can be hard to decipher test results, especially for multiple tests. (This is why you should ask your doctor to explain test results.)

Because areas of cognitive weakness can overlap in different diagnoses, no two children have exactly the same blend of skills and challenges. Barbara Arrowsmith, founder of Canada's neuroplasticity-based Arrowsmith schools, and author of *The Woman Who Changed Her Brain*, gives a broad cognitive test to incoming pupils.[134] The Arrowsmith School test looks at 19 different cognitive areas in the brain and measures them for weakness. Arrowsmith says that, in 30 years of giving this test, no two children's results have been the same.

The medical industry knows that it has a naming and labeling problem with learning differences. In 2001, two authors proposed a new naming scheme called "Atypical Brain Development," that "could be used to address the full range of developmental disorders that are found to be overlapping much of the time."[135] Other doctors have come up with the term "Specific Learning Difficulties," to talk about the overlap between different LDs.[136] And parents report that doctors have told them that many learning and focus challenges might be tied to brain immaturity.[137]

Although we continue to use terms such as dyslexia, dysgraphia, and ADHD, you can use Appendix A to identify which cognitive weaknesses make up your child's diagnosis. More information helps you help your child.

Brain Maturity and Academics

Thirty years ago in the UK, according to Sally Goddard Blythe, director of the UK's Institute for Neuro-Physiological Psychology (INPP), every child was assessed by a doctor at the start of school. Each child was asked to do simple physical tasks such as stand on one leg, hop to the end of the room and back, and pile some bricks; and each child had their sight and hearing tested. The movement test helped to determine whether a child was ready for school.[138] Most schools no longer give physical tests to determine if children are mature enough to start Kindergarten.

Children are tested every year at the doctor's office. As your child visits her pediatrician, the pediatrician checks milestones,[139] to make sure she is developing properly.[140] There is wiggle room in individual milestones, but if there is a pattern of missed milestones, it is cause for taking another look. Although they aren't available to most people yet, doctors are working to put together tests to identify possible learning differences at very early ages.[141]

Many children with LD appear bright and normal at pediatric visits and are given only a cursory milestone examination by a doctor. It's only later on, when LD appears, that parents look backwards and see a pattern. And some children will just hide or camouflage weaknesses.

The important thing to know about both milestones and foundational stages is that, as Lawrence Cutner, Ph.D., says, "The fact that a child passes through a particular developmental stage is always more important than the age of that child when he or she does it."[142] Many reference books that talk about brain development say that certain milestone skills appear before age 5, yet it's common for parents of LD children to report that their children lag behind in acquiring the skills, sometimes by several years.

What are Foundational Skills?

In the year or so before starting Kindergarten, there's an emphasis on developmental milestones that act as *foundational skills* for learning academics. [143] Foundational skills are particularly important, because if a child skips or is very late on developing these skills, it can affect his ability to function and succeed in the academic world.

Foundational skills are often movements that indicate a certain level of brain maturity, or basic skills, like holding a pencil. Goddard Blythe explains that foundational skills provide structural support for higher-level thought. If foundational skills are rocky, it forces other parts of the brain to work harder.

Parents say that it is extremely common for LD children to have missing or late foundational skills, often through grade school and sometimes into middle school. This can result in problems with everything from sitting at a chair, listening, copying from the board, focus, attention, and memory.

For example, if your child is lacking movement-based foundational skills (which have a profound effect on academics, and are explained below), then you have two options. First, you can sit your child at a desk every day, spending hours doing work that is often far too difficult, seeing no progress. Or secondly, you can work with an OT or movement therapist to do fun movements that can help your child achieve a more mature developmental stage, in which he has more foundational skills. With more foundational skills, it's easier to learn

You can teach and practice all of the foundational skills at home. [144] Some children, however, need some extra help learning them. One professional who can help develop foundational skills is an occupational therapist (OT). Other professionals include kinesiologists and movement therapists, as described in Appendix C. Most occupational therapists work with younger children only, often because their tools are designed for smaller bodies. Especially with older children, sports such as gymnastics, karate, and swimming help develop physical foundational skills. And running, jumping, balancing, riding horses, swimming, and swinging are all great ways to develop the brain.

How Do Professionals View Foundational Skills?

The diagram below shows a rough outline of the order in which professionals help foundational skills to develop. This is the basis of many educational programs which incorporate movements, and is often used by professional therapists, whose job it is to help make children succeed.

Because this information is not usually distributed to the public, and there are no agreed-upon terms, many professionals: education professionals, learning specialists, pediatricians, therapists, and specialists, have developed their own diagrams and terminology.

You will see variations of this diagram in other books, but many of the diagrams include ages for when a skill develops. It's important to remember that these skills all develop concurrently, maturing more together each year.

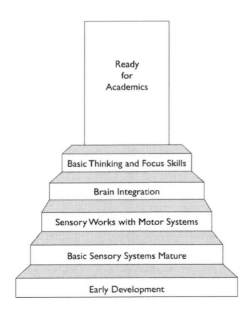

As you work with your child, this diagram can help you set and understand priorities. The top step indicates that your child is fully mature and ready to learn academics. If your child has trouble learning, it's time to start checking down the stairs to the lowest level where skills are missing. Your therapist will start at the lowest level, help the lowest-level skills to develop, and then go up the staircase to learn more skills. Skills on higher-level steps are based upon skills on the lower-level steps, and if low-level skills are missing, it makes it much harder to learn.

The table below explains each step.

Foundational Skills and Movements

The table below lists some examples of the foundational skills that might indicate levels of brain maturity. While the order in these examples may be correct for some children, your child's performance may vary.

On the right side of the table is a list of abilities and *foundational skills*. Many of these skills are measured as milestones. Skills develop in layers, so the base layers are shown at the bottom of the table.

If your child works with an OT or other type of therapist, you can use this chart to talk with the therapist, to better understand what skills your child is developing. You can ask the therapist to explain what skills they are teaching your child, and in what order. You can also use this chart to illustrate to your teacher why certain actions are difficult for your child. It's important to realize that everyone learns how to do almost all of the functions in this table. If your child cannot yet do these functions, all it means is that academics are more difficult for now.

This diagram and chart are meant only to help you understand some of the complex knowledge that therapists deal with, as they work to help your child develop. See www.fineuntilkindergarten.com/bonus for additional resources.

Foundational Stage	*Milestones and Abilities (5+ years of age)*
One Step Below Academic Skills:	• Demonstrates self control
Basic Thinking and Focus Skills	• Can listen and focus • Has developed executive function skills, like problem-solving and setting goals • Can do complex motor skills like dance, catch and throw a ball, and jump rope • Understands stories and can summarize the plot
Brain Integration	• Draws and cuts out a circle or triangle • Holds an item onto paper and traces it • Follows multi-step directions • Can skip, swinging arm opposite knee up • If you draw letters widely across the back, can recognize letters
Sensory Works with Motor Systems	• Can cross the midline of the body (tie shoes, button clothing, cut food) • Can touch each finger to thumb, front and backwards • Stands on one foot (5 sec at 5 yrs; 8-10 sec at 7 yrs) • Eyes follow a finger smoothly in a figure 8
Basic Sensory Systems Mature	• Enjoys sensory experiences, not hypersensitive • Can sit and stand without squirming • Close eyes, get touched on arm, and show on opposite arm where touched. • Draws a figure with at least six body parts
Early Development	• Infant reflexes have disappeared with growth • Sits erect on chair or floor • Healthy

Early development

Early development is shown as the bottom step in the staircase In general, your child should be healthy and settled. By early childhood, your child should be able to sit erect (indicating good core body strength), and the reflexes that your child was born with should have disappeared.

Every child is born with a set of reflexes, which are unconsciously connected movements. An example reflex is, if you lay your finger on the palm of a newborn, the baby grasps your hand. The baby doesn't *consciously decide* to grasp your hand. The baby's brain just responds to stimulus by closing on the finger. Reflexes are actions that aren't routed through the thinking brain. They're just wired in.

When a child's brain develops normally, the brain *integrates* infant reflexes, so they disappear, typically by age two. If you lay your finger into the palm of a typical three-year old, you will no longer see the automatic grasp.

Studies say that over 80% of children who have learning disabilities have *retained* infant reflexes.[145] If you can still measure reflexes in older children, it means that although the brain has developed, it has not fully integrated the reflexes. And many well-established theories say that unintegrated infant reflexes can get in the way of developing foundational skills. One effect of unintegrated reflexes, for example, is toe-walking.[146] Many occupational therapists (OTs), and other movement therapists, use therapy techniques that help infant reflexes integrate—and disappear.

If you think that your child might need help with early development, and if your child has been resistant to learning other movements, even after working with a therapist, you might want to look for a pediatric OT who is trained in reflex integration and will test your child for unintegrated reflexes and offer exercises, because insurance often covers OTs. If you decide to go with a different program, be careful to compare prices and check references.

Basic Sensory Systems Mature

Basic Sensory Systems Mature is the second step. Although we were taught as children that we have five senses—sight, hearing touch, taste, and smell—we actually have far more. Some neurologists say that we have nine senses, and others say that we have over 15. Each sense is connected to its own sensory brain system, responsible for gathering sense information and getting it understood by the brain.

Dr. Jean Ayres developed the *sensory integration* theory (now called *sensory processing*[147]) in the 1950's. In some children, sensory systems develop in an asynchronous fashion, and immature sensory systems can result in children who are at the mercy of their input or the processing of sensory signals. These children often respond to stimulus in an unexpected fashion. Some children are very sensitive to certain types of stimulation, like sound, while others crave stimulation, like movement. These children are often diagnosed with *sensory processing disorder*, and OTs can provide therapies which help the systems develop and integrate.

Two of the sensory systems that are most significant for school performance are the *vestibular system*—also called the sense of balance—and the *proprioceptive system*.

Proprioception comes from the Latin word *proprius*, meaning "one's own," or "individual." Proprioception is the brain's ability to know where its body is in space. A simple way to measure proprioceptive development for your child is to have them balance on one foot with eyes closed. Younger children might have troubles finding their body parts in space. They might also have trouble regulating how much effort it takes to move the body: overshooting or not using enough power.

The vestibular system is closely associated with the inner ear, and helps keep the body balanced. It also helps the body develop clear vision and smooth head movements. The vestibular system ties into postural control, eventually allowing the body to unconsciously keep the body upright while dealing with gravity.

When the vestibular and/or proprioceptive senses are immature, the brain's energy is focused on controlling the body, so the conscious brain must work to keep a child upright and balanced.[148] Ideally, both senses develop before a child starts school, so that his body operates automatically and his brain can focus on classroom lessons. If a child has immature proprioception and vestibular senses, moving can actually help some children focus. When a child moves his body, his movement sends body location information to the brain, freeing up some brain cycles that can then pay attention. This is one of the reasons why the ability to sit still in a classroom is a developmental step, and why some children pay better attention when squirming or rolling around.

Some lower-grade teachers wrap rubber Theraband™ resistance bands around the front legs of children's chairs. This allows the children to bounce their legs off of the bands, giving proprioceptive feedback to the brain and allowing the children to sit and focus.

When the senses are fully developed, the child's movement and body-knowledge is said to be "mind free." This means that the child's brain is free to focus on academics, instead of body management.

Sensory Works with Motor Systems

Sensory Works with Motor Systems is the third step. Your motor systems are a window to your brain maturity. The brain is literally two different pieces. The two sides of the brain are only connected by a small channel called the corpus callosum, inside the brain.

Reaching an arm over to the opposite side of the body is called "crossing the midline." When a child reaches over to the other side of his body, signals pass through the corpus callosum, so that both sides of the brain talk with one another. Crossing the midline comes with brain maturity. Many developmental songs and activities involve practicing this gesture, but some children have a difficult time with it.

Crossing the midline is tied to all sorts of tasks like tying shoes and cutting food with knife and fork. Reaching this level of ability is necessary in order to participate in many classroom activities. Some children are not able to draw a large circle with one arm. They need to draw half of the circle, switch arms, and draw the second half of the circle. These children respond well to OT.

If a child constantly slumps and cannot sit upright, chances are that he has some problems with postural control, which is the convergence of several sensory inputs with the motor system. Some OTs report that most of the children they see have challenges with postural control, which can impact ability to stand, sit, focus, and write.

Brain Integration
Brain Integration is the fourth step. The actions in this section indicate that lower-level systems are mature and are working well together. The ability to skip while swinging the opposite leg is automatic and indicates brain maturity. Together with developing handedness (e.g. becoming right- or left-handed), it's a developmental stage that indicates a child is ready to start school.

Basic Thinking and Focus Skills Basic Thinking and Focus Skills is the top developmental step. It's a good idea to make sure that your child's tutors and teachers understand that if your child hasn't yet reached maturity for some of the lower-level foundational skills, schoolwork is much more difficult.

If your child is having to consciously work to remember where his body is in space and keep his body upright, it's not a huge surprise, for example, if he cannot follow three directions at once.

You can support brain development by doing games that use these actions at home. You can practice standing on one foot with your child. You can play games where she picks up pennies.[149] Learning that physical activity is important for developing the brain— and why—helps parents choose more active lives for their children.

If your child needs to go to a pediatric occupational therapist, you can ask for exercises to do at home—a good OT will happily provide them. You can also support foundational skill development as you parent[150], or by engaging your child in sports. Sally Goddard Blythe's book, *Attention, Balance, and Coordination*, and Carla Hannaford's book, *Smart Moves*, both explain more about foundational skill development and the value of movement in brain development.

Although you might be able to help your child by giving your child therapies, it's important to realize that the brain is extremely complex, and that therapy is rarely an immediate fix for an LD. Therapies and various exercises can help your child's brain to mature, or they can teach a new skill, but you can't always immediately measure outcome in a classroom.

How Do You Start Helping Your Child?

One of the most confusing questions for a parent looking for help is what to do first. When Cara talks about the first few years trying to help her son, she describes it as feeling like one foot was nailed to the ground, while the other foot was running as fast as it could, so she was just going in circles. "My son seemed to need help with everything at the same time: reading, math, handwriting, spelling, social skills, and emotional support. I kept hearing about all of these treatments that seemed to absolutely fix things, but were expensive. I had no idea what should be my highest priorities."

This book already advises you to not go overboard on remedial or therapeutic treatments. It's best to stick with one support activity at a time, although you can work games and activities into your day that can help as well. Remember to help set up an environment in which your child can have fun. As mentioned previously, studies show that stress affects learning.

We suggest choosing how to help your child using two planning methods.

First of all, use the pie method used in businesses. Draw up a list of problems that affect your child's life right now. Then put them into a pie chart. Make the biggest, most important problem be the biggest piece. The problem might be dealing with homework, or getting your child a counselor, or meeting with the principal to adjust how the teacher treats your child. It might also be handwriting, or the ability to read.

Whatever the biggest piece of the pie is, right now—deal with that. Then look at the skill that is the biggest piece of pie. That's the skill to work on for the next two months or so. Use the techniques described in Chapter 3's "Working With Professionals," to set up expectations and deliverables with your child's therapist.

The second method is to look at your child's diagnosis and her foundational skills. Consult a doctor for every concern, particularly concerns like auditory processing problems (need an audiologist), or speech. What's the biggest problem that affects school achievement? Then target that problem and work to overcome it.

Moving
into the Future

In early 2016, I attended a Dyslexia Entrepreneur's Network (DEN) meeting at LucasFilms in San Francisco. (George Lucas is dyslexic.) Because 35% of entrepreneurs are dyslexic, the DEN[151] organization was created to support dyslexic entrepreneurs, and to "change the story of dyslexia, dyscalculia, ADHD and similar labels into one of strengths, not shame. With support, all members of DEN will be able to own who they are, understand it and, best of all, love it."

The DEN meeting was studded with successful people, including Charles Schwab. Each talked about how difficult school had been. The thing that touched me most, however, was a when a panel of entrepreneurs was asked if they had anything else to tell conference attendees. One panelist, a successful out-of-the-box thinker with a string of companies linked to his name, said "I wish my mom had spent less time trying to fix me, and more time letting me make things in the basement."

Just let that sink in for a minute.

No matter what type of learning difference or brain uniqueness your child is experiencing, I hope that this book helps you set up structures and strategies that will let you support and protect your child during the school years.

I also hope this book reminds you to "seize the day." Childhood passes by quickly, and you want your child's memories to include good things: interests, joy, and accomplishments. You can help set up life so that he or she can have protected areas of fun and success.

You are a wonderfully conscientious, hard-working, loving parent. Remember to question things that make your child miserable, and trust yourself to push back or look for options as needed. Very little of our educational system is set in stone, and there are many different ways to learn.

Growing up is not a race. Your child will get there. I wish you great success, and many happy moments that both you and your child will remember with smiles.

APPENDIX A:
What's Inside Your Child's Diagnosis?

Even after sending your child to a professional for a diagnosis, many parents report that they're confused about their child's LD. Sometimes it can take years to understand what a diagnosis really means. Three things to remember:

- You can think of a diagnosis as a set of weaknesses that form a pattern
- Some weaknesses appear in more than one diagnosis
- Children are often diagnosed with more than one LD

In addition to figuring out a diagnosis, parents want to figure out the next steps. How can you translate your child's diagnosis into an action plan for education support or therapy?

This chapter lists the most common diagnoses, in picture form. We've gathered together the most common weaknesses that make up each diagnosis and listed them in each picture. If your child is diagnosed with an LD, you can sit down with your child's test results and your child's doctor, and check off which weaknesses apply to your child. If there are more weaknesses involved, you can add them to the picture. You can also mark which are the most severe weaknesses.

Some weaknesses, such as fine motor skills, executive function, and planning and organization skills, respond well to therapies.[152] Other weaknesses can strengthen with maturity. You can ask your doctor specific questions about how to support each weakness, and you can use this diagram as your work with your teacher to support your child's learning.

For a comprehensive overview of the characteristics of all LDs, see the *Characteristics of Children with Learning Disabilities report,* put out by the National Association of Special Education Teachers[153]. The website www.Understood.com, sponsored by the National Center for Learning Disabilities, has additional information about each type of LD and learning challenge.

The last page of this appendix contains a glossary of terms.

Dyslexia

85% of learning differences are considered dyslexia. Only around ¼ of dyslexics are ever diagnosed. Because dyslexia is a language disorder, not a reading disorder, it affects not just reading, but writing, spelling, processing, perceiving, and attention.

Explicit, systematic, multisensory education, such as Orton Gillingham-based methods, have helped many dyslexic children read and succeed in the school system.

What's Inside of a Dyslexia Diagnosis?

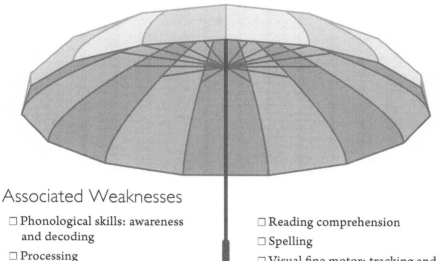

Associated Weaknesses

☐ Phonological skills: awareness and decoding

☐ Processing

☐ Sequencing

☐ Automaticity

☐ Ability to visualize letters

☐ Ability to visualize stories

☐ Oral fluency

☐ Reading comprehension

☐ Spelling

☐ Visual fine motor: tracking and convergence

☐ Working memory

☐ Time awareness and management

☐ Self-organization

May Include:

☐ Handwriting/Dysgraphia

☐ Dyscalculia

☐ ADHD

☐ Executive Function

☐ Immature sensory system

Dysgraphia (Handwriting Disorder)

Dysgraphia can be a big barrier to success in school. Therapy can make a big difference for children with handwriting challenges, and typing accommodations can change failure into success.

Parents sometimes say that stealth dyslexia[154], defined as dyslexia with high reading ability, ends up looking like dysgraphia. Occupational therapy can address many issues with dysgraphia, although not necessarily all.

What's Inside of a Dysgraphia Diagnosis?

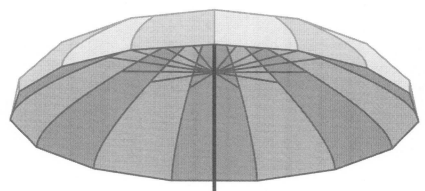

Associated Weaknesses

☐ Visual-spatial (shapes, spacing, writing on line)

☐ Fine motor skills (holding pencil, using scissors)

☐ Visual fine motor (eye teaming, convergence)

☐ Bilateral integration

☐ Language processing

☐ Automaticity

☐ Spelling

☐ Punctuation, capitalization, or grammar

☐ Organization of written language

☐ Hands get tired when handwriting

☐ Working memory

☐ Communicates much better with speech than text

May Include:

☐ Immature sensory system

☐ Executive Function

☐ Dyslexia

Auditory Processing Disorder

Auditory processing disorder (APD) is not yet covered by IDEA, although it is identified by audiologists, teachers, and educational therapists. Many APD children use hearing aids approved through a 504 plan. APD parents often have to work hard to educate teachers on how to support children with APD.

There are some therapies available for APD, but there is no data showing large-scale success.

What's Inside of an Auditory Processing Disorder Diagnosis?

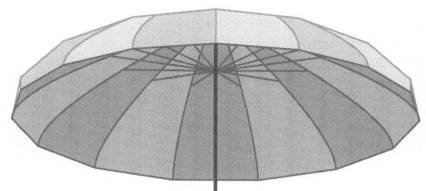

Associated Weaknesses

- ☐ Hearing with background noise
- ☐ Discriminating phonological sounds
- ☐ Speech prosody (rhythm, pitch, and tone)
- ☐ Sound localization
- ☐ Slow auditory processing
- ☐ Auditory memory
- ☐ Auditory closure (the ability to fill in missing parts of sound)

- ☐ Hypersensitive to sound
- ☐ Hard to find speech memories because of poor input
- ☐ Phonological awareness and skills
- ☐ Auditory organizational and sequencing skills
- ☐ Expressive language skills
- ☐ Pragmatic language and social skills

May Include:

- ☐ Social Skills

Dyscalculia (Math Disorder)

This diagram shows some of the skills involved in performing math.[155] Chris Woodin, head of Math Studies at the Landmark School (for dyslexic children), says that when math remediation works best, it "employs the same best practices that are used to address reading struggles."[156]

Therapies provided by an educational therapist can help with dyscalculia weaknesses.

What's Inside of a Dyscalculia Diagnosis?

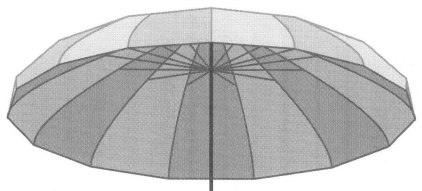

Associated Weaknesses

- ☐ Number sense (sees immediate difference in amounts)
- ☐ Symbol recognition
- ☐ Counting
- ☐ Understanding math terms, operations, and concepts
- ☐ Grouping and sorting
- ☐ Following sequences of steps

- ☐ Memorizing
- ☐ Processing ability and speed
- ☐ Working memory
- ☐ Visual-spatial: lining up numbers correctly
- ☐ Planning and Sequencing
- ☐ Internal idea of time
- ☐ Ability to read a clock

May Include:

- ☐ Immature sensory system
- ☐ Handwriting (dysgraphia)
- ☐ Executive Function

ADHD

ADHD diagnosis can be difficult. Many parents use the Whole-Child Method of diagnosis, described in Appendix C, to rule out causes like allergies, auditory processing disorder or sensory integration.

This diagram lists common weaknesses associated with a diagnosis of ADHD. Many of these weaknesses can be strengthened through exercise and therapy, including cognitive behavior therapy (CBT).

What's Inside of an ADHD Diagnosis?

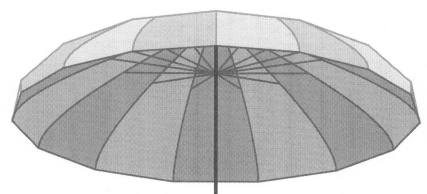

Associated Weaknesses

☐ Self-regulation

☐ Short attention span: distractible

☐ Impulse control: consciously inhibits actions

☐ Task switching

☐ Working memory

☐ Problems regulating: loudness, energy, emotions

☐ Self-organization (neatness)

☐ Time awareness

☐ Verbal self instruction: talks self through problems

☐ Self motivation: setting and working towards goals

☐ Problems listening to and following directions

May Include:

☐ Executive function

☐ Immature sensory system

Executive Function Disorder

Executive function disorder is the ability to identify a goal and work towards it. Some specialists say that executive function disorder has more of an effect on success than ADHD.

Weaknesses in the executive function diagnosis can be exercised by working with a therapist or tutor.

What's Inside of a Executive Function Disorder Diagnosis?

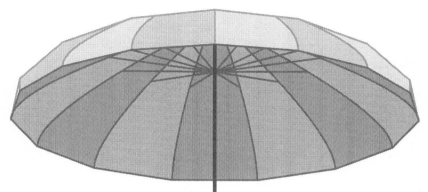

Associated Weaknesses

☐ Identifying the big picture

☐ Planning: setting and prioritizing goals, creating steps

☐ Problem-solving

☐ Goal-driven self-motivation

☐ Sustained attention: follow-through, and attention to detail

☐ Memory: encoding, retrieval, processing, and working memory

☐ Coordinating different actions

☐ Self-organization: neatness, and integrating new information

☐ Time awareness and management

☐ Cognitive flexibility: Can change approach or perspective

☐ Self-monitoring: tracking progress and checking work

May Include:

☐ Social Skills   ☐ ADHD

Social Skills

Social skills are important. About 75% of students with learning differences also have problems with social skills.[157] The ability to get along with others is one of the keys to success in the world.

Investing in a social skills class can be a huge benefit to a child. For more information, see "Speech and Language" in Appendix C.

What's Inside of a Social Skills Problem Diagnosis?

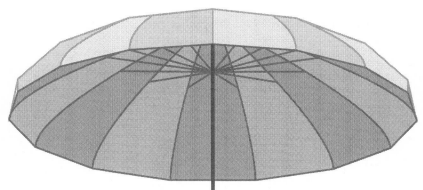

Associated Weaknesses

- ☐ Initiating or joining a conversation or play activity
- ☐ Understanding social cues, e.g. body language and facial expressions
- ☐ Predicting what will happen as a result of action.
- ☐ Understanding things that are implied but not stated explicitly
- ☐ Adapting language, tone, and volume to different situations
- ☐ Understanding and setting social goals

- ☐ Language skills: expressive or receptive
- ☐ Adjusting emotions and behavior to achieve social goals
- ☐ Making a friend and maintaining a friendship
- ☐ Understanding the perspective of others
- ☐ Resolving conflict or losing in a game
- ☐ Working in a group
- ☐ Self-esteem
- ☐ Anxiety or shyness

May Include:

- ☐ Immature Sensory System
- ☐ ADHD
- ☐ Auditory Processing Disorder
- ☐ Dyslexia
- ☐ Executive Function

Sensory Processing and Immature Sensory Development

Sensory Processing Disorder (SPD) happens when the senses mature unevenly. This can result in discomfort with receiving any form of input, such as vision, auditory, language, taste, and how clothing feels. Many children with LDs experience immature sensory development.

Sensory development issues can affect a child's ability to know where his body is in space, and to move his body. Many activities, such as getting dressed and properly using a knife and fork, require mature sensory processing skills.[158]

If sensory abilities are immature, the brain must actively manage body movement, and even manage balance. A child should be mature enough to free the brain from managing body movement, before starting school. Immature sensory development can affect the ability to listen, concentrate, and act in the classroom. It can also affect the ability to sit quietly, copy things from the board, pay attention, or write.

Occupational or movement therapy can help the sensory system to mature.

What's Inside of a Sensory Processing Disorder Diagnosis?

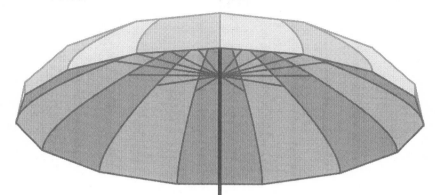

Associated Weaknesses

☐ Overly sensitive to clothing, sounds, touch, vision, or food

☐ Vestibular (e.g. trouble standing on one foot)

☐ Proprioceptive (e.g. trouble learning while sitting still)

☐ Fine and/or gross motor skills

☐ Handedness - hasn't selected dominant hand

☐ Coordination (sports, handwriting, utensils, dressing)

☐ Postural Control (slumps, leans on things)

☐ Clumsy: bumps into things, drops and fumbles, sloppy

☐ Problems regulating: loudness, physicality, emotions

☐ Visual fine motor skills: tracking, focusing

☐ Short attention span: distractible

☐ Problems listening to and following directions

☐ Difficulty with ordinary activities

May Include:

☐ Social Skills

Statistics about Learning Differences

- 70% of children with learning differences exhibit problems with social skills.[159]

- 50% of children diagnosed with ADHD also demonstrate problems with auditory processing disorder.[160]

- 50% of dyslexic children also have ADHD. 35% of children diagnosed with ADHD have dyslexia.[161]

- 50% of dyslexics show difficulties with bilateral integration (like tying shoes), and with motor functions, like handwriting (dysgraphia).[162]

- 25% of dyslexic children have dyscalculia (mathematics). Many children with dyscalculia, however do not have dyslexia.[163]

- 60% of dyslexic children have difficulty with numbers (and 11% excel in numbers)[164]

- It's common for children with dysgraphia to also have dyslexia.

- 75% of children with learning differences have retained infant reflexes. (Described in Chapter 7 in "Foundational Skills and Movements" section.)

Glossary of Terms Used in This Appendix

Auditory memory—A form of short-term memory in which information is heard, processed, stored, and then remembered and used.

Auditory organizational and sequencing skills—The ability to understand and remember the order of words, for example in a sentence.

Automaticity—The ability to do an action as an automatic response, without having to actively think through the steps involved in it.

Bilateral integration—A developmental stage, where a child learns to use both sides of the body together in a coordinated fashion. Used when tying shoes or buttoning.

Comorbidity—A medical term, meaning that a patient has two conditions at the same time.

Convergence—A vision disorder in which the eyes don't work together. Sometimes called "eye teaming." Shows up when looking at items close to the face, when the eyes need to converge on a subject.

Expressive language—The ability to communicate clearly with language. Includes labeling, describing events, forming sentences, using grammar, answering questions, and re-telling stories.

Fine motor skills—The ability to coordinate the eyes and the hands. Includes writing, cutting, tying shoes.

Gross motor skills—The ability to perform large movements of the body, such as running, jumping, and crawling.

Grouping—Trouble understanding that a number (for example, three), applies to any group of three. Problems recognizing groups of three.

Impulse control—The ability to consciously inhibit actions. Also called self-control. Every toddler lacks impulse control. Impulse control grows with maturity, and exercises and therapy can help to develop it.

Integrate—Simple skills are said to develop separately and independently, but are later integrated, or combined into, more complex skills. Integrate is also the process by which the brain collects different types of inputs and combines them.

Internal idea of time—The internal "feeling" for how long five minutes is, and the difference between how long five minutes and a half hour feel, for example.

Language processing—How the brain understands what you hear, and assembles what you want to say.

Neuroplasticity—The brain's ability to change and adapt by forming new neural connections and changing throughout life. Neuroplasticity is involved when a brain compensates for injury, or learns new actions in response to new situations.

Number sense—Ability to see immediate difference in amounts. For example, which is bigger: a group of three, or a group of five?

Organization of written language—The ability to organize information in memory and retrieve it, the ability to think in a structured fashion, and the ability to create outlines, and output, whether through handwriting or typing.

Phonological awareness and skills—The ability to hear sounds that make up words. Includes perceiving rhymes, identifying words that start with the same sound, pointing out smaller pieces of words, and being able to add a letter to create another word.

Phonological sounds—A phonological sound is also called a phoneme. It's a distinct unit of sound in speech. Phonemes string together to make words.

Pragmatic language—The social language that we use to interact with people around us, including both verbal and nonverbal rules. Includes things like how to phrase things, how to position the body, understanding body language and tone. Also called social skills, these skills can be taught. Many LD children need help with social skills.

Processing—The ability of the brain to take in information, reach some judgment on what to do about the information, and then take action. Processing can apply to any type of input.

Proprioception—This sense tells the brain information about where the body is in space. It is involved when we move our limbs without looking at them. An immature proprioceptive sense can result in problems sitting still. Many LD children have problems with proprioception, which can be developed by doing exercises and working with an occupational therapist.

Self-organization—The ability to know where schoolwork is and to retrieve it when necessary. Also used to describe the ability to structure different types of information or pieces of schoolwork, as part of knowing where to start working.

Self-regulation—One of the core strengths of healthy emotional development, the ability to deal with challenging situations in an age-appropriate fashion. Includes tolerating a bit of discomfort or frustration, self-soothing, dealing with transitions, and appropriately controlling emotions and activity levels.

Sequencing—The process of putting events, ideas, and objects in a logical order. Sequencing is a necessary skill for learning counting or the alphabet, being able to prioritize, and being able to follow directions. In math, this might be associated with problems remembering facts and formulas.

Sensory system—The sensory system is responsible for receiving and processing sensory information from the world around you. It includes sensory receptors for vision, hearing, touch, taste, smell, balance, and more. Includes neural pathways, and sensory perception parts of the brain.

Social skills—See "Pragmatic Language," above.

Sorting—The ability to organize items by size, shape, or other characteristics.

Sound localization—The ability to identify where a sound comes from.

Symbol recognition—Ability to identify and remember symbols, to tell the difference between different symbols, and to tell if a symbol is backwards.

Task switching—The ability to switch between different tasks smoothly, without forgetting what you are doing.

Time awareness and management—Common challenge for many LD children. The ability to identify and estimate how long a task will take, and then accomplish the task within the allotted amount of time. Time management skills can be taught.

Tracking—The ability to follow something with the eyes, such as a finger drawing in the air, or a sentence. This is one of the visual fine motor skills that can be improved by working with a developmental optometrist, as described in Appendix C, "The Whole-Child Diagnostic Approach."

Verbal self-instruction—Dr. Russell Barkley, ADHD specialist, talks about the importance of internal language, also called "the mind's voice," and ADHD. He maintains that children with ADHD are delayed in developing the ability to talk themselves through situations. Verbal self-instruction skills can be taught.

Vestibular—The vestibular system determines body balance and movement. The vestibular sense organs are located in the inner ear, and include three semicircular canals, which detect gravity and linear movement. It can be difficult to stand upright or to sit still if the vestibular sense is underdeveloped. Occupational therapy can help to develop this sense.

Visual fine motor—Another term for visual problems that can interfere with reading and education. Includes lazy eye, convergence problems, tracking problems, and so forth. See Appendix C for more information on vision therapy.

Visual-spatial—The ability to see things and relate them to their location, or to distinguish between objects. Can affect motor skills and classroom performance. Occupational therapy can help develop this skill.

Working memory—Also called short-term memory. Stores information that you're currently using. For example, you hold a question in your mind as you turn the page looking for an answer. There are several types of working memory: auditory, visual-spatial, and motor. Working memory increases naturally up until age 12, and can be exercised. *The Mislabeled Child*, by Brock Eide, M.D., M.A., and Fernette Eide, M.D., is the best reference book to inform you about working memory structure.

APPENDIX B:
Symptoms of a Learning Difference

When a professional evaluates your child for an LD, they will only spend a short amount of time with your child. In order to get the best results from an evaluation, it helps to think about what might indicate an LD in your child's behavior, and inform the testing professional. Many different tests are used to identify LDs, and your observations might help determine which tests are used with your child. The checklist in this appendix gives an example of LD symptoms found after Kindergarten.

Many of the symptoms in this checklist may be things that you'll naturally see in younger children, or that every child demonstrates from time to time. When any checklist says "Makes careless mistakes," doctors aren't talking about the type of careless mistake that every child occasionally makes. They're talking about a very obvious pattern of careless mistakes. Some parents suggest that it's a good idea to mentally add the phrase "at a clinical level" to the end of each sentence.

While information in this appendix is from reputable sources, please make sure that you work with qualified professionals to diagnose your child.

Symptoms Shared by Many LDs

Here are some of the first things that parents report noticing, often far before their child is diagnosed with an LD.

- ☐ Appears bright, articulate, and intelligent but cannot read, write, or spell at grade level.
- ☐ Often labeled lazy, dumb, "not trying hard enough," or careless.
- ☐ Problems paying attention
- ☐ Has a hard time following directions
- ☐ Has a hard time staying organized
- ☐ Information seems to go in one ear and out the other
- ☐ Has problems dealing with transitions or new situations
- ☐ Talented in art, building things, imagination, sports, or music
- ☐ Trouble understanding words or concepts
- ☐ Inconsistent: knows one day and doesn't remember on other days. Or learns but forgets five minutes later
- ☐ Unusual trouble in team sports
- ☐ Even when your child tries hard, his performance doesn't reflect his effort
- ☐ Learns best through hands-on experience
- ☐ Takes longer to learn things
- ☐ Mistakes and symptoms increase with stress, time pressure, tiredness, or hunger.

Motor Skills

- ☐ Seems inappropriately clumsy
- ☐ Poor hand-eye coordination

☐ Trouble with buttons, zippers, snaps, scissors, and learning to tie shoes

☐ Dislikes and avoids writing and drawing

☐ Cannot draw a figure with six body parts by first grade

☐ Difficulty coloring within the lines or drawing triangles or squares.

☐ Holds pencil in an unusual fashion

☐ Has a hard time picking up puzzle pieces, coins, or using tweezers

Language

☐ Trouble modulating voice (too loud or too soft)

☐ Trouble remembering names of people or objects

☐ Has difficulty staying on topic

☐ Inserts invented words in conversation

☐ Has difficulty summarizing what has just been said

☐ Uses vague language and has a limited vocabulary

☐ Speech is slow and halting, using lots of fillers (um, er)

☐ Poor grammar, or misuses significant number of words

☐ Mispronounces common words frequently

☐ Confuses similar words or speech sounds

☐ Often has slips of tongue (e.g., a rolling stone gathers no moths)

☐ Has trouble rhyming, cannot tell if two words rhyme

☐ Slowness in learning songs.

☐ Isn't interested in books or stories

☐ Has trouble understanding directions and needs repetition

☐ Has trouble understanding simple word jokes

☐ Cannot easily identify theme or ideas in a story

☐ Cannot tell a simple story using full sentences by first grade.

Reading

☐ Avoids reading or melts down instead of reading

- ☐ Cannot remember the alphabet song
- ☐ Slow to recognize and name letters
- ☐ Confuses similar-looking letters and/or numbers
- ☐ Has problems associating letters and sounds
- ☐ Has a harder time reading short words (is, to, of) than long words (birthday, dinosaur)
- ☐ Reverses letter order in words (e.g., was and saw)
- ☐ Trouble recognizing phonemes: (e.g., first or middle sound in simple words like "bed")
- ☐ Loses place while reading
- ☐ Reads very slowly
- ☐ Problems blending sounds
- ☐ Guesses instead of sounding words out, especially with short words
- ☐ Cannot recognize letter drawn on back (e.g., "X")
- ☐ Has poor memory for story if self-reads, but a good memory if read to
- ☐ Trouble spelling, or cannot spell nonsense words

Written Language

- ☐ Dislikes and avoids writing
- ☐ Unusual difficulty learning to write
- ☐ Trouble writing the same letter in the same way twice
- ☐ Frequently reverses numbers, letters, and symbols
- ☐ Writing is messy, with many mistakes and corrections
- ☐ Unusual difficulty in spelling
- ☐ Trouble copying accurately, from near point, far point, or both
- ☐ Uneven spacing between letters and words, cannot write on the line
- ☐ Trouble seeing problems and correcting work
- ☐ Trouble organizing thoughts into a paragraph

☐ Consistent trouble with capitalization, punctuation, and grammar.

☐ Strong verbal answers to problems, but written answers are just a few words

☐ Leaves words unfinished or omits them when writing sentences

☐ Complains of being tired when writing

Math and Numbers

☐ Has trouble with simple counting of objects

☐ Dislikes board games, or games that require math skills

☐ Number sense (which is bigger, 2 or 6?)

☐ Problems memorizing multiplication and division

☐ Skip counting is difficult (e.g., 2, 4, 6)

☐ Cannot write numbers in columns to do math

☐ No internal idea of time

☐ Cannot do mental math (addition or subtraction)

☐ Avoids games that require strategy

☐ Can read words, but has difficulty reading numbers or remembering a sequence of numbers

☐ Trouble understanding sequences (first we do this, then that)

☐ Difficulty verbally describing math processes

☐ Difficulty remembering telephone numbers.

Brain-Body

☐ Overly energetic and physically active: jumping, spinning, running all the time.

☐ Cannot sit still

☐ Extremely low energy and sedentary

☐ Impulsive behavior

☐ Short attention span: highly distractible

☐ Problems performing coordinated actions: cutting with knife, buttoning, handwriting

☐ Low muscle tone, floppy muscles: hard not to slump

☐ No dominant hand established by age 5, frequently switches hands for activities

☐ Problems with self-regulation: too active, overly emotional

☐ Trouble distinguishing left from right

☐ Sensitive to noises, crowds, lights, clothing

☐ Extreme dislike for normal behavior: bathing, brushing teeth, cutting nails, getting dressed

☐ Very picky eater

☐ Poor balance. Cannot stand on one foot

☐ Consistently covers one eye

☐ Problems with eye contact (not always just an Autism indicator. Can be ADHD, sensory, or visual)

Memory and Cognition

☐ Problem remembering days of the week and months of the year

☐ Excellent memory for experiences, locations, or faces

☐ Poor memory for sequences, facts, and information that hasn't been experienced

☐ Thinks in pictures, not words

☐ Doesn't talk self through problem situations

Appendix D list types of doctors who can test children who exhibit these symptoms for an LD. In general, if you see problems with motor skills or brain-body, you might want to have your child tested by an occupational therapist. A pediatrician can recommend you to an occupational therapist for testing.

APPENDIX C:
The Whole-Child Diagnostic Approach

"Read! Listen! Seek! Question! Find out as much as you can about your child'sdisorder ... question everything. Be prepared to abandon every theory or hypothesis that does not stand up to critical scrutiny."

— Dr. Russell Barkley, *Taking Charge of ADHD: The Complete and Authoritative Guide for Parents*

Because there can be an overlap in different types of problems[165] for children who learn differently, experts and parents agree that it's best to test several different brain systems when diagnosing the cause of learning differences. Parents call this the *whole child diagnostic approach*. A whole-child approach for learning differences involves talking with several different types of professionals and working to put together a view of your whole child.

Many parents report that it took several years for them to realize that they should look at different aspects of their child's learning, as measured by different professionals. Often, the parents had gotten all of their information about the child from one professional, just studying one set of skills. This section gives you an idea of what other parents are looking at.

Appendix D, "Types of Doctors," contains more information on which types of doctors can perform which diagnoses.

- **Vision and Hearing.** Up to 25% of children aged 5 to 17 have a vision problem, and it's estimated that at least 1.4 million children, ages 18 or younger, have hearing problems. If your child demonstrates any problems in school, make sure that they have been tested for both.

- **Speech and Language.** From 5 to 10% of children have trouble understanding language or expressing themselves. If your child isn't expressing himself or responding well, it's a good idea to test speech and language abilities. A *speech-language pathologist,* or *speech therapist* can also test and help with social skills. Many children with ADHD, sensory processing problems, or other learning differences need help with social skills.

- **Trouble hearing or understanding speech.** Auditory processing disorder is a problem with processing hearing input that affects about 5% of school-aged children. APD can affect a child's communication, academics, and social skills. If you suspect APD, you should first give your child a hearing exam. If your child has problems with receptive language or listening comprehension (often detected by a *speech-language pathologist* or a school psychologist), an *audiologist* should screen for APD.

- **Movement and Brain Maturity.** When diagnosing your child for an LD, it turns out that movement examinations are as valuable, perhaps more so, than the traditional block tests and matching games given by neuropsychologists and educational testers. Movement tests can help identify undeveloped foundational skills—the basis for all academic abilities, as described in Chapter 7, "What They Don't Tell You About Learning Differences."

  - *If you find a generalist or a group of doctors who will test your child, make sure that they do a movement (also called a neuro-motor) test, for almost any educational challenge. An pediatric occupational therapist*

(OT) can give a full movement exam as well. You can also request this from your school, in which case you can either request a full OT test, or a handwriting test.

- **Full Educational Evaluation.** If you're asking your school to test your child, you should request a formal psycho-educational evaluation. A formal assessment for learning disabilities includes evaluation of cognition, memory functions, attention, intellectual ability, information processing, psycholinguistic processing, expressive and receptive language function, academic skills, executive function, social-emotional development, and adaptive behavioral functioning.[166]

  - *An educational specialist can give a full picture of a child's cognitive strengths and weaknesses.*

  - *A neuropsychologist can also give a full picture of a child's cognitive strengths and weaknesses, and they can also test for other conditions, such as autism or nonverbal learning disorder.*

  - *In general, neither of these doctors gives a movement exam.*

- **Executive Function Problems.** Specialists are starting to point to executive function (EF) issues as a core problem for many children with LD and ADHD. Executive Function is the ability to create goals, and then sustain actions and problem solving to achieve those goals.[167] In a school setting, you can request an executive function assessment, but many school psychologists are not qualified to give these tests.[168] The school might test your child's working memory and processing speed, but an EF test will also assess planning, the ability to make transitions, and organizational skills. A neuropsychologist can test for EF.

- **Allergies and Digestive Problems.** These are common tests when you're concerned about focus or behavior issues. Does your child have food sensitivities and is he getting proper nutrients? An *allergist* is a medical doctor who can test for allergies, and you can talk with your child's pediatrician about digestive worries. A *registered dietician nutritionist (RDN)* is a credentialed professional who is also able to test for allergies. Appendix D contains a link for finding a RDN.

If your child has chronic diarrhea or problems with vomiting, it might be a good idea to talk with a *pediatric gastroenterologist*. Studies[169] are just starting to research connections between symptoms of LD and ADHD and gut health.[170] There is no information that tells you exactly what to do, but in general, good gut health will potentially improve your child's school performance.

- **Visual Fine Motor Skills**: If your child has trouble reading, a *developmental optometrist* (different from a standard optometrist) checks eye function and eye movement problems, like eye tracking. Like an OT, they will sometimes prescribe movement or vision therapies to help train the brain. Move your finger in front of your child's eyes, from one side to the other. Can your child track the finger smoothly? If his eyes track jerkily (for example) you may want to get him evaluated.

- **Behavioral Issues**. A *psychologist* can be used to test for behavioral issues and anxiety. Psychologists sometimes host social skills groups (see also Speech-Language-Pathologists above and in Appendix D.) *Psychologists* provide therapies. *Psychiatrists* prescribe medication.

- **Parenting Advisor or Parenting Counselor**. Some parents who are worried about their child's behavior meet with a parenting advisor. The advisor comes to the school and to their home, observes their child in several situations, and then gives suggestions to the parents, sometimes including parenting classes. Remember: you can drastically change your child's behavior by changing your parenting.

Very few doctors look at everything in this list, but an *Integrative Pediatrician* looks at many different factors when she examines your child. Be very careful when you choose specialists. Always work with a medical doctor.

Appendix D lists types of doctors and specialists, and includes information about which specialists can diagnose LD or ADHD. Remember to ask up front if a specialist is qualified to issue a diagnosis. If you are getting an alternative diagnosis for an IEP, remember to ask for an independent educational evaluation (IEE) before hiring an outside doctor, if you want the school to pay for the exam. See "Asking for an Independent Educational Evaluation," in Chapter 5. You

There are often multiple causes for behavior, including parenting styles, maturity, anxiety, environment, and learning differences, so jumping to conclusions about a diagnosis without a medical evaluation can be misleading and dangerous.

might also want to talk with other parents, to see if there were any problems accepting an outside diagnosis from this particular doctor or type of practitioner.

APPENDIX D:
Types of Doctors and Specialists

When parents first start trying to help their child, they often think that their pediatrician will handle everything. When I sat down to write this book, I wanted to make sure to include a table showing all of the different specialists and what they do.[171] This list continues to grow, and lists the typical types of doctors and specialists who can help diagnose or support your child.

Professional	What They Do	License/Education	What They Diagnose
School Psychologist	Assesses learning and school problems. Provides therapy. Trained to do intellectual and educational testing. Can assess emotional functioning.	PhD or MA NASP[172]	LD: yes, ADHD: no
School Counselor	Counseling and help with school problems. Many schools no longer have one	ACSA[173]	LD: no, ADHD: no
Special Education Teacher	Teacher trained in identifying and teaching children with learning disabilities.	MA in Special Ed, NASET, different for states.[174]	Identifies, but doesn't diagnose
Education Specialist, also called Learning Specialist	Assesses learning abilities and can perform various functions, including teaching, tutoring, advising on a child's educational needs, and other roles.	Not licensed. (Note: there's also an Ed.S. degree)	May be part of a team LD: not alone, ADHD: no
Educational Therapist	No specific training required. Often have special education training and teaching experience, and training in specific methodologies. Sometimes is mentored by a school-based specialist.	Not licensed. Often has a MA. AET[175]	LD: no, ADHD: no

Professional	What They Do	License/Education	What They Diagnose
Occupational Therapist (should be Pediatric Occupational Therapist)	Specialist identifying and working with sensory, motor, and movement problems. The OT evaluates, and then sets up goals and works toward them in every session.	AA, MA, or Ph.D., In schools and private practice NBCOT[176] Additional certification in various therapies.	LD: some, ADHD: no, Sensory Processing Disorder: yes, Reflex integration issues: yes, depending on training
Speech Language Pathologist (SLP)	Specialist diagnosing and treating speech and language problems. SLP often diagnose and treat feeding problems, auditory problems, and social skills issues, as well. Often, a SLP will offer a social skills class, where children can practice social skills with other children.	MA. In schools and private practice ASHA[177] Additional certification in various therapies.	LD: not alone, ADHD: no
Physician (e.g. Pediatrician)	Medical doctor	State medical board certification ABP[178]	LD: no, ADHD: yes Can prescribe medication
Educational Psychologist	Provides educational testing. Some can provide assessment of cognitive, intellectual functioning as well. Needs Ph.D. to administer a "level C" test (most intellectual functioning tests). Not trained to assess emotional functioning.	MA or Ph.D. for private practice NASP[179]	LD: yes, ADHD: yes

Professional	What They Do	License/Education	What They Diagnose
Clinical Psychologist	Assesses intellectual and emotional functioning. Provides therapy for emotional and behavioral problems. Treats both individuals and groups. In general, does not do educational testing needed to diagnose LD.	Ph.D. and licensing for private practice NASP[180]	LD: no, ADHD: yes
Neuropsychologist	Ph.D. level psychologist who assesses brain processing and functioning. May not be skilled in administering educational tests. Does not typically assess emotional functioning. Often, does not perform a full movement-based neurodevelopmental exam on a child, so it's a good idea to also get an evaluation from an OT. An OT evaluation is good input for a neuropsychologist.	Ph.D. and licensing for private practice ABPP[181]	LD: yes, but may need educational assessment from education specialist, and sensory/motor assessment from occupational therapist. ADHD: yes
Psychiatrist	Medical doctor specializing in diagnosis and treatment of mental health. A psychiatrist is often used to prescribe medication to children.	Certified. ABPN [182]	LD: no, ADHD: yes Can prescribe medication
Audiologist	Clinical expert with a Ph.D. or Au.D. who is expert in the anatomical structures of the middle and inner ear. Performs diagnostic tests to discover extent of damage and pinpoint cause.	National certification. ASHA	LD: auditory processing, ADHD: no

Professional	What They Do	License/Education	What They Diagnose
Developmental Optometrist	Optometrist plus completed post-graduate training & credentialing. Measures visual fine motor skills (oculomotor control) & can prescribe vision therapy for things like vision tracking and focusing. Brought in if symptoms indicate that vision deficits other than near or far-sightedness are affecting a child's functional performance. Optometrists are medical-school educated. Opthamologists are not.	Post-grad work and certification COVD[183]	LD: no, ADHD: no, problems with vision input and processing: yes
Kinesiologist	A kinesiologist is a movement therapist, much like an occupational therapist. Kinesiologists are more popular in Europe. Although occupational therapists are often paid for by US insurance, kinesiologists are not.	KFRP[184]	LD: no, ADHD: no, Sensory Processing Disorder: yes, Reflex integration issues: yes
Movement Therapist	Movement therapist is a generic term. There are many different types of movement therapy, including The Anat Baniel Method©, Bal-a-Vis-X™, Brain Gym®, Masgutova Neurosensorimotor Reflex Integration Method (MNRI®), Theraband™ Rhythmic Movement Training.™ Typically, these therapies require training and certification from the founder.	Certified by the founder of the therapy, at the end of a class series.	LD: no, ADHD: no, Sensory Processing Disorder: partially, Reflex integration issues: yes
Dyslexia Specialist	Dyslexia specialist is a certificate program for general and special education teachers who are trained in Orton-Gillingham methods.	Certification from the Dyslexia Training Institute[185]	

Professional	What They Do	License/Education	What They Diagnose
Educational Consultant	Helps locate and create situations where K-12 students can succeed. Some some specialize in executive function, tools, or college placement.	Usually ed or Psych degrees. Some belong to IECA.[186]	Might have other qualifications that allow diagnosis.
Dietitian, Registered Dietitian Nutritionist (RDN)	Translates science of nutrition into information about everyday diet. Promotes health, educates doctors and clients about nutritional information. Can diagnose food allergies.	BA or MA in Nutrition, 1200 hours of supervised practice, ACEND[187]	LD: no, ADHD: no, Food Allergies: yes, Can perform a nutrition-focused physical exam,[188]
Nutritionist	May have University degree in Food Science or Human Nutrition. Often work for businesses. May work as dietitian assistants or food journalists.	No certification necessary.[189]	

APPENDIX E:
Sample Letters

This appendix contains sample letters. You can also search for sample letters on the internet, or if you belong to an online support group, you can ask parents to forward you letters they have written. It's a good idea to look at one or more sample letters before writing your own.

Chapter 5 of this book explains why we strongly suggest that you begin by asking that your child be tested for an IEP. If your child is having trouble learning, most parents aren't qualified to decide that their child only needs a 504. And there's no consequence and no cost for requesting testing.

This appendix contains four types of sample letters:

- The first letter requests full psycho-educational testing, as part of an official evaluation for an IEP. You will see that we suggest that you give samples of how the teacher has tried to help your child. As we explain in Chapter 5, you should include information that proves your point.

- The second letter requests evaluation for a 504 plan.

- The third letter, asks that the district pay for an outside evaluation. Note that you must get the evaluation approved before you go to an outside doctor, if you want the distict to pay for it.

- The fourth letter is an example of a letter written by a mom to introduce her child to the teacher. You can write one of these to your teacher every year.

Parent's Name
123 Canvas Street
Sunnytown, CA
456-986-9085

October 16, 2016

Principal's Name
Jones Elementary School
Wilson, CA

re: Billy Jones, DOB: 02/03/2010
Grade 2, Mrs. Wilson

Dear [Principal's name],

My name is [your name], and my child [your child's name] is in the __th grade with [name of teacher]. I am writing to request that [your child's name] be given a full psycho-educational evaluation, and be evaluated for services under the Child Find obligations of the Individuals with Disabilities Education Act (IDEA.)

As you may know, my child has been struggling with [List the top things that are the most challenging. Include things like reading, writing, handwriting, paying attention, remembering.] I have spoken with [name of teacher] about these concerns and the following modifications were tried: [Describe what the teacher did to support your child's learning. Examples are: Seated at the front of the room, reminded to pay attention, modified assignments to require less work, kept in at recess to provide extra help.]

I understand that I need to sign a consent so that the school can conduct the evaluation. If I do not hear from you in a week, I will call to set up a time when I can sign the consent form. After testing, and 5 days before any meeting to discuss test results is scheduled, I would like to request that I get to review the test results and ask questions with the evaluator.

I understand that the school district has 60 days to complete testing and hold a meeting to discuss eligibility. I look forward to meeting with you on this date.

Sincerely,

Your Name Here.

Sample Letter: Requesting an IEP

Parent's Name
123 Canvas Street
Sunnytown, CA
456-986-9085

October 16, 2016

Principal's Name
Jones Elementary School
Wilson, CA

re: Billy Jones, DOB: 02/03/2010
Grade 2, Mrs. Wilson

Dear [Principal's name],

My child, [your child's name], has recently been diagnosed with [if your child has received one or more diagnoses, insert them here]. This issue affects his/her ability to learn in the classroom.

My child has been struggling with [List the top things that are the most challenging. Include things like reading, writing, handwriting, paying attention, remembering.]

I have spoken with [name of teacher] about these concerns and the following modifications were tried:[Describe what the teacher did to support your child's learning. Examples are: Seated at the front of the room, reminded to pay attention, modified assignments to require less work, kept in at recess to provide extra help.]

I would like to request that you consider [your child's name] for a 504 plan. I have a list of accommodations, suggested by our doctor, that I would like to request for the classroom.

We look forward to hearing from you and meeting with the 504 team to set up accommodations that will help our child be more successful in school. Thank you in advance for your help.

Sincerely,

Your Name Here.

Sample Letter: Requesting a 504 plan

Parent's Name
123 Canvas Street
Sunnytown, CA
456-986-9085

October 16, 2016

Principal's Name
Jones Elementary School
Wilson, CA

re: Billy Jones, DOB: 02/03/2010
Grade 2, Mrs. Wilson

Dear [Principal's name],

My name is [your name], and my child [your child's name] is in the ___th grade in [name of teacher's] class.

My child, [your child's name], was evaluated for special education services in [month/year.] I am writing to request that the school pay for an Independent Educational Evaluation (IEE) for the following reasons: [CHOOSE ONE OR MORE, or insert your own]

- The school has refused to test my child, even though I have information showing that he or she is not able to learn. [Describe what]
- The evaluation given to my child was incorrect. [Describe how]
- The evaluation wasn't done in my child's native language, or with necessary accommodations. [Describe how]
- The original evaluation was incomplete and additional tests are needed. [Describe how]

I would like to request that the IEE be completed as quickly as possible so that we can set up a program to support [child's name] in school. Please respond as soon as possible and send me copies of the school and district's guidelines for this. My daytime telephone number is: [insert number.]

Thank you,
Sincerely,
[Your Name]
cc: Your district's Director of Special Education
Your district's Superintendent (if you choose)

Sample Letter: Asking the District to Pay for an Independent Educational Evaluation (IEE)

Parent's Name
123 Canvas Street
Sunnytown, CA
456-986-9085

October 16, 2016

Principal's Name
Jones Elementary School
Wilson, CA

re: Billy Jones, DOB: 02/03/2010
Grade 2, Mrs. Wilson

Dear Mrs. Jones,

My name is Sasha, and I'm Rafael Wilson's mom. We are very excited to have you as a teacher this year. One of Rafael's teachers last year suggested that we write his new teacher a note, to summarize some of the things that we have learned are effective.

Teachers have told us (and we can see) that Rafael is a very bright little boy. He's quick verbally, never forgets a story, is artistic, loves to draw and paint, and just loves to be outside. Rafael is a hard worker. He will work hard on projects, and he loves to do a good job.

Sometimes Rafael gets anxious in the classroom. If this happens, our previous teacher told us that she let him go to the bathroom, or clean up around the classroom, and that moving helped him.

Rafael has been diagnosed with dyslexia, dysgraphia, and low working memory, so he is entering your classroom with an IEP.

The IEP goals are: [You can talk about your child's IEP Goals.]

In addition, we ask for [add specific accommodations.]

I would like to set up a meeting with you in the next two weeks, so that I can show you some samples of what worked well for us last year. In the meantime, if there is anything I can do to support your teaching efforts, please let me know.

Thank you,

Sasha Wilson

Sample Letter: Letter Introducing Your Child

Acknowledgements

This book is the result of a ten-year journey in which my husband and I learned how to support our own unique learner. Thank you to Scott Wiener and my family for their support and never boring, always amusing company along the way.

Thank you to Nathalie Cowan, for mothering me through this manuscript, and being a great friend. Thanks to Caryn Coleman and Phillip Gessert for their help with the manuscript. Thanks to my mother, Ruth Mikkelsen, for bringing her school principal perspective to this book. And thanks to Agnes Charrel-Berthillier, for the years spent working on the BrainParenting vision of bringing information to parents.

I have worked with communities and information since my days at NeXT Computer, and I have many people to thank for their efforts along the way. In particular, I want to thank the people I know who have worked to help parents share information with one another. It's important. Ginger Ogle, the original founder of the 10,000-member Berkeley Parents Network; Susan Walton, who founded the Peninsula Parents of Special-Needs Kids; and Shannon Des Roches Rosa and Jennifer Byde Myers, who founded The Thinking Person's Guide to Autism.

Notes

Chapter 1

1. "Early Identification." *LD Online* http://www.ldonline.org/article/c673

2. Thomas Armstrong, Ph.D., "The Myth of the Normal Brain: Embracing Neurodiversity." *AMA Journal of Ethics, April 2015* http://journalofethics.ama-assn.org/2015/04/msoc1-1504.html

3. Thomas West, "Amazing Shortcomings, Amazing Strengths." *Asia Pacific Journal of Developmental Differences, 2014* http://www.landmark.edu/m/uploads/ T._West_Hidden_Talents_Dyslexia.pdf

4. For the most part, we use the term "learning difference" to correspond with the disorders listed in the Individuals with Disabilities Education Act (IDEA), which designates a *specific learning disability* as "a disorder in one or more of the basic psychological processes involved in understanding or in using language, spoken or written, that may manifest itself in the imperfect ability to listen, think, speak, read, write, spell, or to do mathematical calculations." This disability category includes dyslexia. Almost half of all LD children fall into the category of SLD. ADHD is protected under Section 504 of the Rehabilitation Act of 1973 (Section 504) and the Americans with Disabilities Act of 1990 (ADA). The Office for Civil Rights in the U. S. Department of Education enforces the provisions of Section 504 and Title II of the ADA with respect to school districts, while the Department of Education administers IDEA.

5. "Causes of Learning Disabilities." *National Association of Special Education Teachers (NASET)* https://www.naset.org/3864.0.html

6. Cheryl Silver, Ronald Ruff, et al., "Learning disabilities: The need for neuropsychological evaluation." *Archives of Clinical Neuropsychology*, Volume 23, Issue 2, March 2008 http://www.ncbi.nlm.nih.gov/pubmed/17977692

7. British Dyslexia Association

8. "How many people are affected/at risk for learning disabilities?" *US Department of Health and Human Services, Eunice Kennedy Shriver National Institute of Child Health and Human Development* https://www.nichd.nih.gov/health/topics/learning/conditioninfo/pages/risk.aspx, and Center for Disease Control and Prevention, "Mental Health in the United States: Prevalence of Diagnosis and Medication Treatment for Attention-Deficit/Hyperactivity Disorder." *Morbidity and Mortality Weekly Report*, 2005 https://www.cdc.gov/mmwr/preview/mmwrhtml/mm5434a2.htm

9. "The State of Learning Disabilities." National Center for Learning *Disabilities* http://www.ncld.org/wp-content/uploads/2014/11/2014-State-of-LD.pdf

10. Larry Silver, M.D., "Related Disorders of a Learning Disability: What You Should Know." *Learning Disabilities Association of America* https://ldaamerica.org/what-you-should-know-about-related-disorders-of-learning-disability/

11. Karen Rogers, Ph.D., "Thinking Smart About Twice Exceptional Learners: Steps for Finding Them and Strategies for Catering to Them Appropriately." *Dual Exceptionality*, Australian Association for the Education of the Gifted and Talented web book http://www.aaegt.net.au/DEEWR%20Books/DE%20Final%20Compile.pdf

12. "Children and Youth with Disabilities." *National Center for Education Statistics* http://nces.ed.gov/programs/coe/indicator_cgg.asp

13. "Types of Learning Disabilities." *Learning Disabilities Association of America* https://ldaamerica.org/types-of-learning-disabilities/

14. Gina Kemp, M.A., Melinda Smith, M.A., and Jeanne Segal, Ph.D. "Learning Disabilities and Disorders." *Helpguide.org* http://www.helpguide.org/articles/learning-disabilities/learning-disabilities-and-disorders.htm

15. "Social Skill Deficits and Learning Disabilities: A Meta-Analysis." *Kaval* http://ldx.sagepub.com/content/29/3/226.abstract

16. Robert Slavin, Nancy Karweit, and Barbara Wasik, "Preventing Early School Failure: What Works?" *ACSD Educational Leadership* http://www.ascd.org/publications/educational-leadership/dec92/vol50/num04/Preventing-Early-School-Failure@-What-Works%C2%A2.aspx

17. Brock Eide, M.D., M.A., and Fernette Eide, M.D., *The Dyslexic Advantage, Unlocking the Hidden Potential of the Dyslexic Brain.*

18. "Study Advice: Understanding Dyslexia and Dyspraxia." *University of Hull* http://www2.hull.ac.uk/student/pdf/StudyAdvice-dyswhatunderstanding.pdf

19. Dr. Fernette and Dr. Brock Eide, authors of "The Dyslexic Advantage: Unlocking the Hidden Potential of the Dyslexic Brain." *Wired Magazine Q and A*, 2011 http://www.wired.com/2011/09/dyslexic-advantage/

20. Julie Logan, "Dyslexic Entrepreneurs: The Incidence; Their Coping Strategies and Their Business Skills." *Wiley InterScience* website. http://www.nota.nu/sites/default/files/Dyslexic_Entrepreneurs_Logan.pdf

Chapter 2

21. Amy Arnsten, Ph.D., Carolyn Mazure, Ph.D., et al., "Neural circuits responsible for conscious self-control are highly vulnerable to even mild stress. When they shut down, primal impulses go unchecked and mental paralysis sets in." *Scientific American*, April, 2012 http://www.ncbi.nlm.nih.gov/pmc/articles/PMC4774859/

22. The IEP and 504 plans are described in Chapter 6, School Support Programs for LD."

23. Nalavany, Carawan, and Brown, 2011, "Considering the role of traditional and specialist schools: do school experiences impact the emotional well-being and self-esteem of adults with dyslexia?" *British Journal of Special Education* http://onlinelibrary.wiley.com/doi/10.1111/j.1467-8578.2011.00523.x/abstract

24. Gale Morrison, Ph.D., Merith Cosden, Ph.D., "Risk, Resilience, and the Adjustment of Individuals with Learning Disabilities." *Learning Disability Quarterly*, February 1997 http://www.ldonline.org/article/Risk,_Resilience,_and_Adjustment_of_Individuals_with_Learning_Disabilities?theme=print

25. David Bernstein, "How schools (even great ones) fail kids with ADHD." *The Washington Post*, 2012 https://www.washingtonpost.com/blogs/answer-sheet/post/how-schools-even-great-ones-fail-kids-with-adhd/2012/09/23/8e81c83c-f828-11e1-8253-3f495ae70650_blog.html

26. Slavin, Karweit, & Wasik, "Preventing Early School Failure: What Works?" *ACSD Educational Leadership*, December, 1992 http://www.ascd.org/publications/educational-leadership/dec92/vol50/num04/Preventing-Early-School-Failure@-What-Works%C2%A2.aspx

27. "Providing Appropriate Education for Students with Learning Disabilities in Regular Education Classrooms.: American Speech-Language-Hearing Association (ASHA) Position Statement: National Joint Committee on Learning Disabilities http://www.asha.org/policy/PS1991-00101/

28. Thomas Armstrong, "Neurodiversity" excerpt from "The Power of Neurodiversity: Unleashing the Advantages of Your Differently Wired Brain." *American Institute for Learning and Human Development* http://www.institute4learning.com/neurodiversity.php

29. Alfie Kohn, author of "Unconditional Parenting," "Five Reasons to Stop Saying 'Good Job!'" http://www.alfiekohn.org/article/five-reasons-stop-saying-good-job/

30. Melissa Dahl, "That Grade School Was (Probably) Right to Dump Homework." NY Magazine, March 2015 http://nymag.com/scienceofus/2015/03/that-grade-school-was-right-to-dump-homework.html

31. "Research Spotlight on Homework: NEA Reviews of the Research on Best Practices in Education." National Education Association http://www.nea.org/tools/16938.htm

32. Harris Cooper and Barbara Nye, "Homework for Students with Learning Disabilities: The Implications of Research for Policy and Practice," *Journal of Learning Disabilities*, 1994 http://ldx.sagepub.com/content/27/8/470.abstract

33. "What research says about the value of homework: At a glance," *Center for Public Education* http://www.centerforpubliceducation.org/Main-Menu/Instruction/What-research-says-about-the-value-of-homework-At-a-glance

34. "Brain Matures a Few Years Late in ADHD, But Follows Normal Pattern" *National Institute of Mental Health* https://www.nih.gov/news-events/news-releases/brain-matures-few-years-late-adhd-follows-normal-pattern

35. "The State of Learning Disabilities: Facts, Trends, and Emerging Issues" *National Center for Learning Disabilities* http://www.ncld.org/wp-content/uploads/2014/11/2014-State-of-LD.pdf

36. Kimberly Twyman, M.D., Conway Saylor, Ph.D., "Bullying and ostracism experiences in children with special health care needs," *Journal of Developmental and Behavioral Pediatrics*, 2010 http://www.ncbi.nlm.nih.gov/pubmed/20081430

37. Wrightslaw website, *Bullying and Harassment*, http://www.wrightslaw.com/info/harassment.index.htm

38. Sigal Saban "Teach Your Child Social Skills Lesson #4: Help Your child Understand the Difference between Rudeness, Meanness, and Bullying," *The Mom and Dad Academy* http://momanddadacademy.com/2014/07/teach-child-social-skills-help-child-understand-difference-rudeness-meanness-bullying/

39. Cheryl Marsiglia, Ph.D., Jeffrey Walczyk, Ph.D., Walter Buboltz, Ph.D., Diana Griffith-Ross, "Impact of Parenting Styles and Locus of Control on Emerging Adults' Psychosocial Success." *Journal of Education and Human Development*, Vol. 1, Issue 1, 2007 http://www.scientificjournals.org/journals2007/articles/1031.htm

40. Dr. Russell Barkley, Ph.D., "Essential Ideas for Parents" speech in front of Center for ADHD Awareness, Canada (CADDAC), July 13, 2012 *CADDAC* https://www.youtube.com/watch?v=SCAGc-rkIfo

41. Betty Osman, Ph.D., "How Learning Disabilities Affect a Child's Siblings." *Great Schools* http://www.greatschools.org/gk/articles/learning-disabilities-and-siblings/

42. Edward Hallowell, Ph.D., "Their Beautiful Minds." *Dr. Hallowell,* http://www.drhallowell.com/blog/their-beautiful-minds/

Chapter 3

43. Marshall Raskind, Ph.D., and Roberta Goldberg, Ph.D., "Life Success for Students with Learning Disabilities." *LDOnline* 2005 http://www.ldonline.org/article/12836/

44. Jaime Casap, Chief Education Evangelist, Google, "My Speech for FLOTUS' 'Beat the Odds' Summit at the White House July 23, 2015," *Education Evangelist* http://eduevangelist.blogspot.com/2015/07/ my-speech-for-flotus-beat-odds-summit.html

45. "Student Voices: A Study of Young Adults with Learning and Attention Issues." 2015 National Council for Learning Disabilities http://www.ncld.org/wp-content/ uploads/2015/08/Student-Voices-Executive-Summary.pdf

46. KJ Dell'Antonia, "Age-Appropriate Chores for Children (and Why They're Not Doing Them)," *New York Times Motherlode*, 2014 http://parenting.blogs.nytimes.com/2014/01/27/ age-appropriate-chores-for-children-and-why-theyre-not-doing-them/?_r=0

47. Laura Grace Weldon, "How Kids Benefit from Chores." *Wired Magazine*, June 15, 2012 http://www.wired.com/2012/06/chores-benefit-kids/

48. "Evaluating Health Information." *Medline Plus and National Institute of Health,* 2016 https://medlineplus.gov/evaluatinghealthinformation.html

49. Paola Bonifaccci, Ph.D., Michele Storti, MS, et al., "Specific Learning Disorders: A Look Inside Children's and Parent's Psychological Well-Being and Relationships." *Journal of Learning Disabilities*, 2015 http://www.ncbi.nlm.nih.gov/pubmed/ 25609675

50. Peter Gray, Ph.D., *Free to Learn: Why Unleashing the Instinct to Play Will Make Our Children Happier, More Self-Reliant, and Better Students for Life*, 2001

51. "Children and TV: Limiting your child's screen time." *Mayo Clinic Children's Health*, August 6, 2016 http://www.mayoclinic.org/healthy-lifestyle/childrens-health/ in-depth/children-and-tv/art-20047952

52. Karen Waggoner, M.Ed., Lorraine Wilgosh, Ph.D., "Concerns of Families of Children with Learning Disabilities." *Journal of Learning Disabilities*, February 23, 1997 website *http://ldx.sagepub.com/content/23/2/97.abstract*

53. Keith Crnic, Catherine Gaze, and Casey Hoffman, "Cumulative Parenting Stress Across the Preschool Period: Relations to Maternal Parenting and Child Behaviour at Age 5." *Infant and Child Development*, 2005

54. Beth Berry, "In the Absence of the Village, Mothers Struggle Most." *Revolution from Home* 2016 blog http://revolutionfromhome.com/2016/04/ absence-village-mothers-struggle/

55. Sherry Latson, "Preventing Parent Burn Out: Model for Teaching Effective Coping Strategies to Parents of Children with Learning Disabilities." *Learning Disabilities Association of America newsletter*, August 14, 2014 https://hr.ucsf.edu/ hr.php?A=1077&AT=&org=we

56. A good example of a private support group is Northern California's Peninsula Parents of Special Needs Kids, founded by Susan Walton http://www.ppsnk.org/

57. Berkeley Parents Network website is public, but you need to enroll to ask or answer questions. https://www.berkeleyparentsnetwork.org/

58. Peninsula Parents of special-needs kids is a group for special-needs children in Northern California. http://www.ppsnk.org/

Chapter 4

59. Linda Blanton, Marleen Pugach, Lani Florian, "Preparing General Education Teachers to Improve Outcomes for Students with Disabilities." *National Center for Learning Disabilities* http://www.ncld.org/wp-content/uploads/2014/11/aacte_ncld_recommendation.pdf

60. "Child Find." *Wrightslaw* website, http://www.wrightslaw.com/info/child.find.index.htm

61. "Understanding FAPE." *Understandingspecialeducation.com* http://www.understandingspecialeducation.com/fape.html

62. Shannon Pedigo Efteland quotation, from *Dysgraphia Facebook forum*, August, 2016

63. Here's an example Pinterest website that displays examples of what number sense means: the ability to visualize and really understand a quantity. "Math Anchor Posters." *We Are Teachers* Pinterest page https://www.pinterest.com/weareteachers/math-anchor-charts-number-sense/

64. *Developing Learning Profiles* http://inclusive.tki.org.nz/assets/Uploads/Developing+Learner+Profiles+infosheet.pdf

65. Pamela Wright and Peter Wright, "Assessments, Evaluations, Tests." *Wrightslaw.com* http://www.wrightslaw.com/info/test.index.htm

66. Cindy Gaddis' original Yahoogroup is called *Homeschooling Creatively*. The group is no longer active, although you can search the archives if you subscribe here: homeschoolingcreatively-subscribe@yahoogroups.com The group has now moved to a Facebook page at: https://www.facebook.com/TheRightSideofNormal

67. This display gives a sample of the "accommodations" information available on Pinterest, https://www.pinterest.com/search/pins/?q=accommodations&rs=typed&term_meta\[\]=accommodations%7Ctyped

68. "Classroom Accommodations and Modifications Checklist for APD." *Auditory Integration Training* website (Note: inclusion of this checklist is not a recommendation for AIT therapy.) http://www.aitinstitute.org/auditory_processing_classroom_modifications.htm

69. This page, titled "A 504 Plan for Those with Dyslexia," lists many good accommodations for dyslexia. You can use these accommodations in either a 504 plan, or in an IEP. For more information, see Chapter 6 of this book. *Orton Gillingham Online Tutor* http://www.ortongillinghamonlinetutor.com/504-plan-dyslexia/

70. There is a collection of sensory integration accommodations and ideas on Pinterest. https://www.pinterest.com/search/pins/?q=sensory%20integration%20accommodations%20and%20ideas&rs=typed&term_meta%5B%5D=sensory%20integration%20accommodations%20and%20ideas%7Ctyped

71. Susan Jones, "Dysgraphia Accommodations and Modifications." *LD Online* http://www.ldonline.org/article/6202/

72. "List of Appropriate School-Based Accommodations and Interventions, for a 504 plan or for adaptations and modifications section of an IEP." *Assistive Technology Training Online Project (ATTO)*, University of Buffalo School of Public Health and Health Professions http://www.aitinstitute.org/auditory_processing_classroom_modifications.htm

73. Teresa Kellerman, "504 Accommodation Checklist." *Fetal Alcohol Syndrome and Fetal Alcohol Spectrum Disorders* website, http://www.come-over.to/FAS/IDEA504.htm

Chapter 5

74. David Flink is also author of *Thinking Differently, An Inspiring Guide for Parents of Children with Learning Disabilities*. (William Morrow 2014)

75. In October of 2015, the US Department of Education sent a letter out to school districts, telling them that they should use the terms "dyslexia," "dysgraphia," and "dyscalculia" in IEPs, in IEP meetings, and in evaluations. Geri Coleman Tucker, "US Department of Education Encourages Schools to Use the Terms "Dyslexia," "Dysgraphia," and "Dyscalculia" in IEPs." *Understood.org* https://www.understood.org/en/community-events/blogs/in-the-news/2015/10/23/us-department-of-ed-encourages-schools-to-use-the-terms-dyslexia-dysgraphia-and-dyscalculia-in-ieps

76. In July of 2016, the US Department of Education sent a letter telling school districts that they need to support ADHD, and that sometimes, ADHD qualifies for IEP support, not just Section 504. The government is telling school districts to support these LDs. "Dear Colleague" Letter from the US Department of Education, Office for Civil Rights, to schools, dated July 26, 2016 *US Department of Education* http://www2.ed.gov/about/offices/list/ocr/letters/colleague-201607-504-adhd.pdf

77. Russell Barkley, Ph.D., *Taking Charge of ADHD*, has a full description of "being an executive parent."

78. "Resources for Parents." *National Dissemination Center for Children with Disabilities* http://www.parentcenterhub.org/wp-content/uploads/repo_items/bp3.pdf

79. "Find Your Parent Center." *Center for Parent Information and Resources* http://www.parentcenterhub.org/find-your-center/

80. Amanda Morin, "Understanding the Full Evaluation Process," *Understood.org* https://www.understood.org/en/school-learning/evaluations/evaluation-basics/understanding-the-full-evaluation-process

81. "Prior Written Notice" section of the "Guidance on Required Content of Forms Under Part B of the IDEA, *U.S. Department of Education* website, page 1, http://idea.ed.gov/download/modelform_Procedural_Safeguards_June_2009.pdf

82. "How to know if your child's making progress toward IEP goals," *GreatKids* http://www.greatschools.org/gk/articles/making-progress-toward-iep-goals/

83. Matt Foley, M.Ed., and DeAnn Hyatt-Foley, M.Ed., "Ten Common Mistakes Parents Make During the IEP Meeting." *Kids Together* http://www.kidstogether.org/IEP/iepd-10-mistakes.htm

84. Pat Howey, "Can the IEP Team Prepare a "Draft IEP" Before an IEP Meeting?" *Wrightslaw* http://www.wrightslaw.com/info/iep.draft.howey.htm

85. Kristin Stanberry, "The IEP Meeting: An Overview." *Understood* https://www.understood.org/en/school-learning/special-services/ieps/the-iep-meeting-an-overview

86. "Characteristics of Children with Learning Disabilities." *NASET LD Report #3 National Association of Special Education Teachers* http://www.naset.org/fileadmin/user_upload/LD_Report/Issue__3_LD_Report_Characteristic_of_LD.pdf

87. "Assistive Technology." *Wrightslaw* http://www.wrightslaw.com/info/atech.index.htm

88. G. Bowser and P. Reed, "Considering Your Child's Need for Assistive Technology," *LD Online* http://www.ldonline.org/article/6246/

89. Kristin Stanberry, "Finding Out if Your Child is Eligible for Special Education." *Understood.org* https://www.understood.org/en/school-learning/special-services/special-education-basics/finding-out-if-your-child-is-eligible-for-special-education

90. Andrew M.I. Lee, "The 13 Conditions Covered Under IDEA" lists which disability categories are eligible for IDEA. See "Key Takeaways" on this page. *Understood.org* https://www.understood.org/en/school-learning/special-services/special-education-basics/conditions-covered-under-idea

91. For the most part, we use the term "learning difference" to correspond with the disorders listed in the Individuals with Disabilities Education Act (IDEA), which designates a *specific learning disability* as "a disorder in one or more of the basic psychological processes involved in understanding or in using language, spoken or written, that may manifest itself in the imperfect ability to listen, think, speak, read, write, spell, or to do mathematical calculations." This disability category includes dyslexia. Almost half of all LD children fall into the category of SLD. ADHD is protected under Section 504 of the Rehabilitation Act of 1973 (Section 504) and the Americans with Disabilities Act of 1990 (ADA).

92. Pam and Pete Wright, "My Child with a 504 Plan is Failing, School Won't Help: Your Eligibility Game Plan." *Wrightslaw* http://www.wrightslaw.com/info/sec504.idea.eligibility.htm

93. Matt Foley, M.Ed., L.P.C., and DeAnn Hyatt-Foley, M.Ed. "Ten Common Mistakes Parents Make During the IEP Meeting." *Kids Together, Inc nonprofit* http://www.kidstogether.org/IEP/iepd-10-mistakes.htm

94. Institute of Education Sciences, *What Works Clearinghouse* http://ies.ed.gov/ncee/wwc/

95. Pete Wright and Pam Wright "Wrightslaw Game Plan: Smart IEPs." *Wrightslaw* http://www.wrightslaw.com/info/iep.goals.plan.htm

96. Companion website to book *From Emotions to Advocacy*: http://www.fetaweb.com/

97. Pam and Pete Wright, "Smart IEPs." *From Emotion to Advocacy* http://www.wrightslaw.com/bks/feta2/ch12.ieps.pdf

98. Kristin Stanberry, "Understanding 504 Plans." *Understood.org* https://www.understood.org/en/school-learning/special-services/504-plan/understanding-504-plans

99. "Can a School be Forced to Evaluate a Child?" *Wrightslaw* http://www.wrightslaw.com/info/test.force.school.htm

100. Pam Wright, "Can the District Limit What They Will Pay for an IEE?" *Wrightslaw* website blog, http://www.wrightslaw.com/blog/can-the-district-limit-what-they-will-pay-for-an-iee/

101. Pam and Pete Wright, "My Child with a 504 Plan is Failing, School Won't Help: Your Eligibility Game Plan." *Wrightslaw* website blog http://www.wrightslaw.com/info/sec504.idea.eligibility.htm

102. "When Teachers Won't Provide Accommodations in the IEP." *Wrightslaw* http://www.wrightslaw.com/blog/when-teachers-wont-provide-accommodations-in-the-iep/

103. "Special Education: Numbers of Formal Disputes are Generally Low and States are Using Mediation and Other Strategies to Resolve Conflicts." *United States General Accounting Office* http://www.gao.gov/new.items/d03897.pdf

104. DVD "Surviving Due Process: Stephen Jeffers v. School Board," *Wrightslaw* http://www.wrightslaw.com/store/dpdvd.html

105. Download of instructions for writing a due process request letter or a state complaint, *Wrightslaw* http://www.wrightslaw.com/video/dueprocessrequestvideo.htm

106. "IDEA Special Education Due Process Complaints/Hearing Requests: A Guide for Parents of Children and Youth (Ages 3-21)." *Office of Special Education Programs, US Department of Education* http://www.directionservice.org/cadre/pdf/DueProcessParentGuideJAN14.pdf

107. "Help! I Need Some Support at the IEP Meeting" *Wrightslaw* http://www.wrightslaw.com/blog/help-i-need-some-support-at-the-iep-meeting/

Chapter 6

108. Annie Stuart "Early Intervention: What it is and How it Works." *Understood.org* https://www.understood.org/en/learning-attention-issues/treatments-approaches/early-intervention/early-intervention-what-it-is-and-how-it-works

109. Kristin Stanberry, "Understanding 504 Plans." *Understood* https://www.understood.org/en/school-learning/special-services/504-plan/understanding-504-plans

110. The Understood Team "The Difference Between IEPs and 504 Plans." *Understood.org* https://www.understood.org/en/school-learning/special-services/504-plan/the-difference-between-ieps-and-504-plans

111. "Responsiveness to Intervention and Learning Disabilities." *National Joint Committee on Learning Disabilities* http://www.ldonline.org/article/11498?theme=print

112. "The Important of Response to Intervention (RTI) in the Understanding, Assessment, Diagnosis, and Teaching of Students with Learning Disabilities." *NASET LD Report #5 National Association of Special Education Teachers* http://www.naset.org/fileadmin/user_upload/LD_Report/Issue__5_LD_Report_Importance_of_RTI.pdf

113. Edward Schultz, Cynthia Simpson, and Sharon Lynch, "Specific Learning Disability Identification: What Constitutes a Pattern of Strengths and Weaknesses?" *Learning Disabilities Association of America* http://ldaamerica.org/wp-content/uploads/2013/10/Journal-Vol-18-2_article.pdf

114. "Key Issues in RTI Implementation," *Educational Research Newsletter and Webinars* http://www.ernweb.com/educational-research-articles/key-issues-in-rti-implementation/

115. "A Parent's Guide to Response to Intervention," *Understood.org* https://www.understood.org/en/school-learning/special-services/rti/e-book-a-parents-guide-to-response-to-intervention-rti

116. Patricia Jones, "Reduction of Referrals to Special Education through Response to Interventions and Differentiated Instruction." *Northern Michigan University* https://www.nmu.edu/education/sites/DrupalEducation/files/UserFiles/Jones_Patricia_MP.pdf

117. Nancy Bailey, Ph.D., "Response to Intervention—An Excuse to Deny Services to Students with Learning Disabilities?" *Living in Dialogue* blog http://www.livingindialogue.com/response-intervention-excuse-deny-services-students-learning-disabilities/

118. Jeff Martin, "The RTI Hurdle," *The Wrightslaw Way* blog http://www.wrightslaw.com/blog/the-rti-hurdle/

119. Sarah Sparks, "Study, RTI Practice Falls Short of Promise." *Education Week*, 2015 http://www.edweek.org/ew/articles/2015/11/11/study-rti-practice-falls-short-of-promise.html

120. Martin, "The RTI Hurdle." *The Wrightslaw Way* blog http://www.wrightslaw.com/blog/the-rti-hurdle/

121. Kristin Stanberry, "Understanding Individualized Education Programs." *Understood.org* https://www.understood.org/en/school-learning/special-services/ieps/understanding-individualized-education-programs

122. ibid., "Understanding Individualized Education Programs," *Understood.org* https://www.understood.org/en/school-learning/special-services/ieps/understanding-individualized-education-programs\#item0

123. Kristen Stanberry, "The Process of Getting Your Child an IEP." *Understood.org* https://www.understood.org/en/school-learning/special-services/ieps/the-process-of-getting-your-child-an-iep

124. Andrew M.I. Lee, "The 13 Conditions Covered Under IDEA." *Understood.org* https://www.understood.org/en/school-learning/special-services/special-education-basics/conditions-covered-under-idea

125. www.fineuntilkindergarten.com

126. www.fineuntilkindergarten.com

127. Sheryl Frishman, "Ten Reasons Why You Should Have an Advocate for Your Child with Special Needs." *Friendship Circle* http://www.friendshipcircle.org/blog/2012/08/20/ten-reasons-why-you-should-have-an-advocate-for-your-child-with-special-needs/

Chapter 7

128. Thomas West, "Understanding the Hidden Talents of Dyslexics." *Creativity and Growth* https://stateoftheart.creatubbles.com/2015/10/08/understanding-the-hidden-talents-of-dyslexics/

129. Susan Hall, "Is it a Reading Disorder or Developmental Lag?" *LDOnline* http://www.ldonline.org/article/32540/

130. Emilio Ferrer, "Early Intervention in Dyslexia Can Narrow Achievement Gap." *Journal of Pediatrics* 2015

131. Talbot F, Pepin, M Loranger M, "Computerized Cognitive Training with Learning-Disabled Students." website

132. Kenneth Kavale and Steven Forness, "The Politics of Learning Disabilities." *LDOnline* http://www.ldonline.org/article/6106/

133. Laura Markson, "ADHD Comorbidities are the Rule, Not the Exception." *Orion School Blog* http://the504school.blogspot.com/2010/11/adhd-comorbidities-are-rule-not.html

134. "Description of Learning Dysfunctions addressed by the Arrowsmith Program." *Arrowsmith Program Background* http://www.arrowsmithschool.org/arrowsmithprogram-background/ld-descriptions.html

135. Jeff Gilger, Ph.D., B. Kaplan, "Atypical brain development: a conceptual framework for understanding developmental learning disabilities." *Developmental Neuropsychology*, 2000 website

136. Pamela DePonio, University of Edinburgh, "Dyslexia and Co-occurring Specific Learning Difficulties." *Let's Read, Reading and Print Disabilities in Young People*, Talinn, Estonia, 2012 http://www.ifla.org/files/assets/libraries-for-print-disabilities/conferences-seminars/2012-08-tallinn/2012-08-08-deponio.pdf

137. Arthur R. Jensen, "Understanding Readiness: An Occasional Paper." *ERIC Clearinghouse on Early Childhood Education*, 1969 http://eric.ed.gov/?id=ED032117

138. Sheila Wayman "How Creeping and Crawling Influence Children's First Step in Education." The Irish Times, June 2, 2015 http://www.irishtimes.com/life-and-style/health-family/parenting/how-creeping-and-crawling-influence-children-s-first-step-in-education-1.2225493

139. "Developmental Checklists: Birth to Five." *Early Childhood Direction Center, Women and Children's Hospital of Buffalo, New York,* 2006, http://www.preschoollearningcenter.org/images/upload/developmental_checklist.pdf

140. "Developmental Milestones." *Center for Disease Control and Prevention* http://www.cdc.gov/ncbddd/actearly/milestones/index.html

141. Kelli Johnson, "Rapid Automatized Naming Tests: What You Need to Know." *Understood.org* https://www.understood.org/en/school-learning/evaluations/types-of-tests/rapid-automatized-naming-tests-what-you-need-to-know

142. Lawrence Kutner, Ph.D., "The Truth About Developmental Milestones." *Psych Central* http://psychcentral.com/lib/the-truth-about-developmental-milestones/

143. "School Readiness Checklist." *Suffolk Early Childhood Development Commission* http://www.suffolkecdc.com/families/school-readiness/school-readiness-checklist/

144. Tracey le Roux, "Occupational therapy versus Therapy Activities at Home." *OT Mom's Learning Activities* website and ebooks http://www.ot-mom-learning-activities.com/occupational-therapy.html

145. Sally Goddard Blythe, "Neurological Dysfunction as a Significant Factor in Children with Dyslexia," *The Institute for Neuro-Physiological Psychology (INPP)* download PDF at http://www.oepf.org/sites/default/files/journals/jbo-volume-12-issue-6/12-6%20Goddard.pdf

146. Whole Child Learning Solutions, "Empowering Parents and Teachers to Optimize the Brain Development of their Children." *Tonic Labyrinthine Reflex* http://www.wholechildlearningsolutions.com/tonic-labyrinthine-reflex-tlr1.html

147. Roseanna Schaff, Ph.D., OTR/L, FAOTA, and Lucy Jane Miller, Ph.D., OTR, and Executive Director, SPD Foundation, "Occupational Therapy Using a Sensory Integrative Approach for Children with Developmental Disabilities," *SPD Foundation* https://www.ncbi.nlm.nih.gov/pubmed/15977314

148. R. Nicolson, A Fawcett, "Automaticity, a new framework for dyslexia research?" *Cognition,* 1990 https://www.ncbi.nlm.nih.gov/pubmed/2354611

149. Christie Kiley, MA, OTR/L, "25 Fine Motor Activities Using Household Items." *Mama OT* http://mamaot.com/fine-motor-activities-using-household-items/

150. Tracey le Roux, "OT Learning Activities for Kids." *OT Mom* http://www.ot-mom-learning-activities.com/

151. http://denlaunch.com/

Appendix A

152. "Research in Brain Function and Learning: Facts about Brain Development and Learning" *American Psychological Association* http://www.apa.org/education/k12/brain-function.aspx

153. "Characteristics of Children with Learning Disabilities." NASET LD Report #3, *National Association of Special Education Teachers* http://www.naset.org/fileadmin/user_upload/LD_Report/Issue__3_LD_Report_Characteristic_of_LD.pdf

154. Stealth Dyslexia Resources, *Dyslexia Advantage* http://community.dyslexicadvantage.org/group/stealth-dyslexia

155. Chris Woodin, "Demystifying Math Struggles & Identifying Strategies to Help," *The Yale Center for Dyslexia and Creativity* http://dyslexia.yale.edu/math.html

156. Liane Kaufman, Ao. Prof. Dr., Vichael Von Aster, Prof. Dr. med. "The Diagnosis and Management of Dyscalculia." *Deutsches Arzteblatt International* http://www.ncbi.nlm.nih.gov/pmc/articles/PMC3514770/

157. Kenneth Kavale, Ph.D., "Social Skill Deficits and Learning Disabilities: A Meta-Analysis." *Journal of Learning Disabilities*

158. *Sensory Processing Disorder* website: http://www.sensory-processing-disorder.com/child-behavior-problems.html

159. Kenneth Kavale, Steven Forness, "Social Skill Deficits and Learning Disabilities: a Meta-Analysis." *Journal of Learning Disabilities*, 1996 https://www.ncbi.nlm.nih.gov/pubmed/8732884

160. Cynthia Riccig, "Relationship between ADHD and Central Auditory Processing Disorder." *School Psychology International* 1996

161. Linda Spiro, Psy.D., "The Most Common Misdiagnoses in Children," *Child Mind Institute* http://childmind.org/article/the-most-common-misdiagnoses-in-children/

162. Marshall Gladstone, Catherine Best et al., "Anomalous bimanual coordination among dyslexic boys." *Developmental Psychology*, 1989

163. M. Huc-Chabrolle, MA Barthez et al, "Psychocognitive and psychiatric disorders associated with developmental dyslexia: a clinical and scientific issue." *Encephale*, 2010

164. British Dyslexia Association

Appendix C

165. For more information, see "Every Child has a Different Profile of LD Challenges," in Chapter 7, *What They Don't Tell You About Learning Differences.*

166. "Learning Disabilities, Dyslexia, and Vision." *American Academy of Pediatrics* http://pediatrics.aappublications.org/content/124/2/837

167. Dr. Russell Barkley, Ph.D., "The Important Role of Executive Functioning and Self-Regulation in ADHD©" *Russell Barkley* website: http://www.russellbarkley.org/factsheets/ADHD_EF_and_SR.pdf

168. "School-Based Assessment of Executive Functions." *Center on Brain Injury Research and Training* http://cbirt.org/tbi-education/assessment-eligibility/school-based-assessment-executive-functions/

169. This is a comprehensive, but complex article talking about the connection between gut health the behavior. Augusto Montiel-Castro, Rina González, Gabriela Bravo-Ruiseco, and Gustavo Pacheco-López, "The microbiota-gut-brain axis: neurobehavioral correlates, health, and sociality," *Frontiers in Integrative Neuroscience,* October 7, 2013, http://www.ncbi.nlm.nih.gov/pmc/articles/PMC3791857/

170. David Kohn, "When Gut Bacteria Changes Brain Function," *The Atlantic magazine,* June 24, 2015 http://www.theatlantic.com/health/archive/2015/06/gut-bacteria-on-the-brain/395918/

Appendix D

171. Table uses input from a table developed by Kathleen Ross-Kidder, Ph.D., director of LD Online. http://www.drc.calpoly.edu/content/eligibility/whoCanDiagnose

172. "State Credentialing Requirements." *National Association of School Psychologists (NASP)* https://www.nasponline.org/standards-and-certification/state-school-psychology-credentialing-requirements

173. "State Certification Requirements."*American School Counselor Association (ACSA)* https://www.schoolcounselor.org/school-counselors-members/careers-roles/state-certification-requirements

174. "Board Certification in Special Education." *National Association of Special Education Teachers (NASET)* https://www.naset.org/2457.0.html

175. "Educational Therapy Defined." *Association of Educational Therapists* https://www.aetonline.org/EducationalTherapyDefined.html

176. "Certification Eligibility Requirements." *National Board for Certification in Occupational Therapy (NBCOT)* http://www.nbcot.org/certification-candidates-eligibility

177. "Certification." *American Speech-Language-Hearing Association (ASHA)* http://www.asha.org/certification

178. "What is Certification?" *American Board of Pediatrics* https://www.abp.org/content/what-certification

179. "State School Psychology Credentialing Requirements." *National Association of School Psychologists (NASP)* https://www.nasponline.org/standards-and-certification/state-school-psychology-credentialing-requirements

180. "National Certification." *National Association of School Psychologists (NASP)* https://www.nasponline.org/standards-and-certification/national-certification

181. "Definition of a Clinical Neuropsychologist." *American Board of Professional Psychology (ABPP)* http://www.abpp.org/i4a/pages/index.cfm?pageid=3304

182. "Check Physician Status." *American Board of Psychiatry and Neurology, Inc. (ABPN)* website www.abpn.com

183. "About COVD." *College of Optometrists in Vision Development (COVD)* http://www.covd.org/?page=About_Us

184. "Practitioner Search." *Kinesiology Federation Registered Professionals (KFRP)* http://www.kinesiologyfederation.co.uk/search/

185. *Dyslexia Training Institute* http://www.dyslexiatraininginstitute.org/index.html

186. *Independent Educational Consultants Association* http://www.iecaonline.com/

187. *Accreditation Council for Education in Nutrition and Dietetics* http://www.eatrightacend.org/ACEND/

188. Carrie Dennet, MPH, RDN, CD, "Nutrition-Focused Physical Exams." *Today's Dietitian*, Vol. 18 http://www.todaysdietitian.com/newarchives/0216p36.shtml

189. The Academy of Nutrition and Dietetics lists state affiliate dietetic associations that can help you find a nutritionist or RDN near you. http://www.eatrightpro.org/resource/membership/academy-groups/affiliates/state-affiliates